**Excerpts from two of the stories:**

From "Shame"

The teacher thought I was stupid. Couldn't spell, couldn't read, couldn't do arithmetic. Just stupid. Teachers were never interested in finding out that you couldn't concentrate because you were so hungry, because you hadn't had any breakfast. All you could think about was noontime, would it ever come? Maybe you could sneak into the cloakroom and steal a bite of some kid's lunch out of a coat pocket.

From "Rowing the Bus"

"You're Georgie's new little boyfriend, aren't you?" he yelled. The hot blast of his breath carried droplets of his spit into my face. In a complete betrayal of the only kid who was nice to me, I denied George's friendship.

"No, I'm not George's friend. I don't like him. He's stupid," I blurted out.

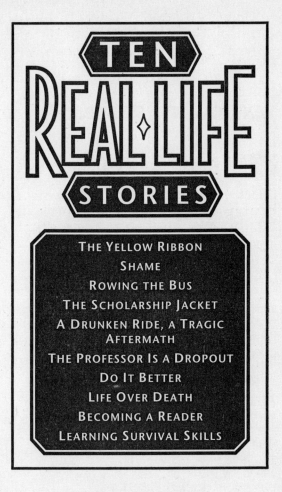

# TEN
# REAL·LIFE
# STORIES

THE YELLOW RIBBON
SHAME
ROWING THE BUS
THE SCHOLARSHIP JACKET
A DRUNKEN RIDE, A TRAGIC
AFTERMATH
THE PROFESSOR IS A DROPOUT
DO IT BETTER
LIFE OVER DEATH
BECOMING A READER
LEARNING SURVIVAL SKILLS

Editor: John Langan
Afterword by Beth Johnson

 THE TOWNSEND LIBRARY

# TEN REAL-LIFE STORIES

**TP** THE TOWNSEND LIBRARY

For more titles in the Townsend Library,
visit our website: **www.townsendpress.com**

All new material in this edition is copyright
© 2006 by Townsend Press.
Printed in the United States of America.

0 9 8 7 6 5 4

Illustrations © 2006 by Hal Taylor

**Townsend Press, Inc.**
**439 Kelley Drive**
**West Berlin, New Jersey 08091**

ISBN-13: 978-1-59194-059-3
ISBN-10: 1-59194-059-1

Library of Congress Control Number:
2005935411

# CONTENTS

## PREVIEW

When America is involved in overseas military actions, US communities often display yellow ribbons to symbolize the hope that their sons and daughters will return home safely. That practice was probably inspired by this story, which first appeared as a newspaper column. Read it to learn what message a yellow handkerchief conveyed to a worried, lonely man.

1

# THE YELLOW RIBBON

*Pete Hamill*

They were going to Fort Lauderdale, the girl remembered later. There were six of them, three boys and three girls, and they picked up the bus at the old terminal on 34th Street, carrying sandwiches and wine in paper bags, dreaming of golden beaches and the tides of the sea as the gray cold spring of New York vanished behind them. Vingo was on board from the beginning.

As the bus passed through Jersey and into

Philly, they began to notice that Vingo never moved. He sat in front of the young people, his dusty face masking his age, dressed in a plain brown ill-fitting suit. His fingers were stained from cigarettes and he chewed the inside of his lip a lot, frozen into some personal cocoon of silence.

Somewhere outside of Washington, deep into the night, the bus pulled into a Howard Johnson's, and everybody got off except Vingo. He sat rooted in his seat, and the young people began to wonder about him, trying to imagine his life: Perhaps he was a sea captain, maybe he had run away from his wife, he could be an old soldier going home. When they went back to the bus, the girl sat beside him and introduced herself.

"We're going to Florida," the girl said brightly. "You going that far?"

"I don't know," Vingo said.

"I've never been there," she said. "I hear it's beautiful."

"It is," he said quietly, as if remembering something he had tried to forget.

"You live there?"

"I did some time there in the Navy. Jacksonville."

"Want some wine?" she said. He smiled and

took the bottle of Chianti and took a swig. He thanked her and retreated again into his silence. After a while, she went back to the others, as Vingo nodded in sleep.

In the morning they awoke outside another Howard Johnson's, and this time Vingo went in. The girl insisted that he join them. He seemed very shy and ordered black coffee and smoked nervously, as the young people chattered about sleeping on the beaches. When they went back on the bus, the girl sat with Vingo again, and after a while, slowly and painfully and with great hesitation, he began to tell his story. He had been in jail in New York for the last four years, and now he was going home.

"Four years!" the girl said. "What did you do?"

"It doesn't matter," he said with quiet bluntness. "I did it and I went to jail. If you can't do the time, don't do the crime. That's what they say and they're right."

"Are you married?"

"I don't know."

"You don't know?" she said.

"Well, when I was in the can I wrote to my wife," he said. "I told her, I said, Martha, I understand if you can't stay married to me. I told her that. I said I was gonna be away a long time, and that if she couldn't stand it, if the kids kept askin' questions, if it hurt her too much, well, she could just forget me. Get a new guy— she's a wonderful woman, really something— and forget about me. I told her she didn't have to write me or nothing. And she didn't. Not for three and a half years."

"And you're going home now, not knowing?"

"Yeah," he said shyly. "Well, last week, when I was sure the parole was coming through I wrote her. I told her that if she had a new guy, I understood. But if she didn't, if she would take me back, she should let me know. We used to live in this town, Brunswick, just before Jacksonville, and there's a great big oak tree just as you come into town, a very famous tree, huge. I told her if she would take me back, she should put a yellow handkerchief on the tree, and I would get off and come home. If she didn't want me, forget it, no handkerchief, and I'd keep going on through."

"Wow," the girl said. "Wow."

She told the others, and soon all of them were in it, caught up in the approach of Brunswick, looking at the pictures Vingo showed them of his wife and three children, the woman handsome in a plain way, the children still unformed in a cracked, much-handled snap-shot. Now they were twenty miles from Brunswick and the young people took over win-dow seats on the right side, waiting for the approach of the great oak tree. Vingo stopped looking, tightening his face into the ex-con's mask, as if fortifying himself against still anoth-er disappointment. Then it was ten miles, and then five and the bus acquired a dark hushed mood, full of silence, of absence, of lost years, of the woman's plain face, of the sudden letter on the breakfast table, of the wonder of children, of the iron bars of solitude.

Then suddenly all of the young people were up out of their seats, screaming and shouting and crying, doing small dances, shaking clenched fists in triumph and exaltation. All except Vingo.

Vingo sat there stunned, looking at the oak tree. It was covered with yellow handkerchiefs, twenty of them, thirty of them, maybe hun-dreds, a tree that stood like a banner of welcome blowing and billowing in the wind, turned into a gorgeous yellow blur by the passing bus. As the young people shouted, the old con slowly rose from his seat, holding himself tightly, and made his way to the front of the bus to go home.

## PREVIEW

Although he was famous first as a comedian, Dick Gregory became equally well known as a social activist. In this excerpt from his autobiography, Gregory gives a glimpse into two incidents from his early life, incidents that helped shape his commitment to aiding the oppressed without insulting their dignity.

# SHAME

*Dick Gregory*

I never learned hate at home, or shame. I had to go to school for that. I was about seven years old when I got my first big lesson. I was in love with a little girl named Helene Tucker, a light-complected little girl with pigtails and nice manners. She was always clean and she was smart in school. I think I went to school then mostly to look at her. I brushed my hair and even got me a little old handkerchief. It was a lady's handkerchief, but I didn't want Helene to

**11**

see me wipe my nose on my hand. The pipes were frozen again, there was no water in the house, but I washed my socks and shirt every night. I'd get a pot, and go over to Mister Ben's grocery store, and stick my pot down into his soda machine. Scoop out some chopped ice. By evening the ice melted to water for washing. I got sick a lot that winter because the fire would go out at night before the clothes were dry. In the morning I'd put them on, wet or dry, because they were the only clothes I had.

Everybody's got a Helene Tucker, a symbol of everything you want. I loved her for her goodness, her cleanness, her popularity. She'd walk down my street and my brothers and sisters would yell, "Here comes Helene," and I'd rub my tennis sneakers on the back of my pants and wish my hair wasn't so nappy and the white folks' shirt fit me better. I'd run out on the street. If I knew my place and didn't come too close, she'd wink at me and say hello. That was a good feeling. Sometimes I'd follow her all the way home, and shovel the snow off her walk and try to make friends with her Momma and her aunts. I'd drop money on her stoop late at night on my way back from shining shoes in the taverns. And she had a Daddy, and he had a good job. He was a paper hanger.

I guess I would have gotten over Helene by

summertime, but something happened in that classroom that made her face hang in front of me for the next twenty-two years. When I played the drums in high school it was for Helene and when I broke track records in college it was for Helene and when I started standing behind microphones and heard applause I wished Helene could hear it, too. It wasn't until I was twenty-nine years old and married and making money that I finally got her out of my system. Helene was sitting in that classroom when I learned to be ashamed of myself.

It was on a Thursday. I was sitting in the back of the room, in a seat with a chalk circle drawn around it. The idiot's seat, the trouble-maker's seat.

The teacher thought I was stupid. Couldn't spell, couldn't read, couldn't do arithmetic. Just stupid. Teachers were never interested in finding out that you couldn't concentrate because you were so hungry, because you hadn't had any breakfast. All you could think about was noontime, would it ever come? Maybe you could sneak into the cloakroom and steal a bite of some kid's lunch out of a coat pocket. A bite of something. Paste. You can't really make a meal of paste, or put it on bread for a sandwich, but sometimes I'd scoop a few spoonfuls out of the big paste jar in the back of the room. Pregnant people get strange tastes. I was pregnant with poverty. Pregnant with dirt and pregnant with smells that made people turn away, pregnant with cold and pregnant with shoes that were never bought for me, pregnant with five other people in my bed and no Daddy in the next room, and pregnant with hunger. Paste doesn't taste too bad when you're hungry.

The teacher thought I was a troublemaker. All she saw from the front of the room was a little black boy who squirmed in his idiot's seat and made noises and poked the kids around him. I guess she couldn't see a kid who made noises because he wanted someone to know he was there.

It was on a Thursday, the day before the Negro payday. The eagle always flew on Friday. The teacher was asking each student how much his father would give to the Community Chest. On Friday night, each kid would get the money from his father, and on Monday he would bring it to the school. I decided I was going to buy a Daddy right then. I had money in my pocket from shining shoes and selling papers, and whatever Helene Tucker pledged for her Daddy I was going to top it. And I'd hand the money right in. I wasn't going to wait until Monday to buy me a Daddy.

I was shaking, scared to death. The teacher opened her book and started calling out names alphabetically.

"Helene Tucker?"

"My Daddy said he'd give two dollars and fifty cents."

"That's very nice, Helene. Very, very nice indeed."

That made me feel pretty good. It wouldn't take too much to top that. I had almost three dollars in dimes and quarters in my pocket. I stuck my hand in my pocket and held onto the money, waiting for her to call my name. But the teacher closed her book after she called everybody else in the class.

I stood up and raised my hand.

"What is it now?"

"You forgot me."

She turned toward the blackboard. "I don't have time to be playing with you, Richard."

"My Daddy said he'd . . ."

"Sit down, Richard, you're disturbing the class."

"My Daddy said he'd give . . . fifteen dollars."

She turned around and looked mad. "We are collecting this money for you and your kind, Richard Gregory. If your Daddy can give fifteen dollars you have no business being on relief."

"I got it right now, I got it right now, my Daddy gave it to me to turn in today, my Daddy said . . ."

"And furthermore," she said, looking right at me, her nostrils getting big and her lips getting thin and her eyes opening wide, "we know you don't have a Daddy."

Helene Tucker turned around, her eyes full of tears. She felt sorry for me. Then I couldn't see her too well because I was crying, too.

"Sit down, Richard."

And I always thought the teacher kind of liked me. She always picked me to wash the blackboard on Friday, after school. That was a big thrill, it made me feel important. If I didn't wash it, come Monday the school might not function right.

"Where are you going, Richard!"

I walked out of school that day, and for a long time I didn't go back very often. There was shame there.

Now there was shame everywhere. It seemed like the whole world had been inside that classroom, everyone had heard what the teacher had said, everyone had turned around and felt sorry for me. There was shame in going to the Worthy Boys Annual Christmas Dinner for you and your kind, because everybody knew what a worthy boy was. Why couldn't they just call it the Boys Annual Dinner, why'd they have to give it a name? There was shame in wearing the brown and orange and white plaid mackinaw the welfare gave to three thousand boys. Why'd it have to be the same for everybody so when you walked down the street the people could see you were on relief? It was a nice warm mackinaw and it had a hood, and my Momma beat me and called me a little rat when she found out I stuffed it in the bottom of a pail full of garbage way over on Cottage Street. There was shame in running over to Mister Ben's at the end of the day and asking for his rotten peaches, there was shame in asking Mrs. Simmons for a spoonful of sugar, there was shame in running out to meet the relief truck. I hated that truck, full of food for you and your kind. I ran into the house and hid when it came. And then I started to sneak through alleys, to take the long way home so the people going into White's Eat Shop wouldn't see me. Yeah, the whole world heard the teacher that day, we all know you don't have a Daddy.

It lasted for a while, this kind of numbness. I spent a lot of time feeling sorry for myself. And then one day I met this wino in a restaurant. I'd been out hustling all day, shining shoes, selling newspapers, and I had googobs of money in my pocket. Bought me a bowl of chili for fifteen cents, and a cheeseburger for fifteen cents, and a Pepsi for five cents, and a piece of chocolate cake for ten cents. That was a good meal. I was eating when this old wino came in. I love winos because they never hurt anyone but themselves.

The old wino sat down at the counter and ordered twenty-six cents worth of food. He ate it like he really enjoyed it. When the owner, Mister Williams, asked him to pay the check, the old wino didn't lie or go through his pocket like he suddenly found a hole.

He just said: "Don't have no money."

The owner yelled: "Why in hell you come in here and eat my food if you don't have no money? That food cost me money."

Mister Williams jumped over the counter and knocked the wino off his stool and beat him over the head with a pop bottle. Then he stepped back and watched the wino bleed. Then he kicked him. And he kicked him again.

I looked at the wino with blood all over his face and I went over. "Leave him alone, Mister Williams. I'll pay the twenty-six cents."

The wino got up, slowly, pulling himself up to the stool, then up to the counter, holding on for a minute until his legs stopped shaking so bad. He looked at me with pure hate. "Keep your twenty-six cents. You don't have to pay, not now. I just finished paying for it."

He started to walk out, and as he passed me, he reached down and touched my shoulder. "Thanks, sonny, but it's too late now. Why didn't you pay it before?"

I was pretty sick about that. I waited too long to help another man.

## PREVIEW

If you could go back in time and undo one thing you are sorry for, what would it be? Such a long-regretted moment is the focus of Paul Logan's essay. While we can never turn back the clock, this story shows how we can do the next best thing: we can turn our regrets into valuable lessons in living.

# ROWING THE BUS

*Paul Logan*

When I was in elementary school, some older kids made me row the bus. Rowing meant that on the way to school I had to sit in the dirty bus aisle littered with paper, gum wads, and spitballs. Then I had to simulate the motion of rowing while the kids around me laughed and chanted, "Row, row, row the bus." I was forced to do this by a group of bullies who spent most of their time picking on me.

I was the perfect target for them. I was small. I had no father. And my mother, though she worked hard to support me, was unable to afford clothes and sneakers that were "cool." Instead she dressed me in outfits that we got from "the bags"—hand-me-downs given as donations to a local church.

Each Wednesday, she'd bring several bags of clothes to the house and pull out musty, wrinkled shirts and worn bell-bottom pants that other families no longer wanted. I knew that people were kind to give things to us, but I hated wearing clothes that might have been donated by my classmates. Each time I wore something from the bags, I feared that the other kids might recognize something that was once theirs.

Besides my outdated clothes, I wore thick glasses, had crossed eyes, and spoke with a persistent lisp. For whatever reason, I had never learned to say the "s" sound properly, and I pronounced words that began with "th" as if they began with a "d." In addition, because of my severely crossed eyes, I lacked the hand and eye coordination necessary to hit or catch flying objects.

As a result, footballs, baseballs, soccer balls and basketballs became my enemies. I knew, before I stepped on the field or court, that I would do something clumsy or foolish and that everyone would laugh at me. I feared humiliation so much that I became skillful at feigning illnesses to get out of gym class. Eventually I learned how to give myself low-grade fevers so the nurse would write me an excuse. It worked for a while, until the gym teachers caught on. When I did have to play, I was always the last one chosen to be on any team. In fact, team captains did everything in their power to make their opponents get stuck with me. When the unlucky team captain was forced to call my name, I would trudge over to the team, knowing that no one there liked or wanted me. For four years, from second through fifth grade, I prayed nightly for God to give me school days in which I would not be insulted, embarrassed, or made to feel ashamed.

I thought my prayers were answered when my mother decided to move during the summer before sixth grade. The move meant that I got to start sixth grade in a different school, a place where I had no reputation. Although the older kids laughed and snorted at me as soon as I got on my new bus—they couldn't miss my thick glasses and strange clothes—I soon discovered that there was another kid who received the brunt of their insults. His name was George, and everyone made fun of him. The kids taunted him because he was skinny; they belittled him because he had acne that pocked and blotched his face, and they teased him because his voice was squeaky. During my first gym class at my new school, I wasn't the last one chosen for kickball; George was.

George tried hard to be friends with me, coming up to me in the cafeteria on the first day of school. "Hi. My name's George. Can I sit with you?" he asked with a peculiar squeakiness that made each word high-pitched and raspy. As I nodded for him to sit down, I noticed an uncomfortable silence in the cafeteria as many of the students who had mocked George's clumsy gait during gym class began watching the two of us and whispering among themselves. By letting him sit with me, I had violated an unspoken law of school, a sinister code of childhood that demands there must always be someone to pick on. I began to realize two things. If I befriended George, I would soon receive the same treatment that I had gotten at my old school. If I stayed away from him, I might actually have a chance to escape being at the bottom.

Within days, the kids started taunting us whenever we were together. "Who's your new little buddy, Georgie?" In the hallways, groups of students began mumbling about me just loud enough for me to hear, "Look, it's George's ugly boyfriend." On the bus rides to and from school, wads of paper and wet chewing gum were tossed at me by the bigger, older kids in the back of the bus.

It became clear that my friendship with George was going to cause me several more years of misery at my new school. I decided to stop being friends with George. In class and at lunch, I spent less and less time with him. Sometimes I told him I was too busy to talk; other times I acted distracted and gave one-word responses to whatever he said. Our class-mates, sensing that they had created a rift between George and me, intensified their attacks on him. Each day, George grew more desperate as he realized that the one person who could prevent him from being completely isolat-ed was closing him off. I knew that I shouldn't avoid him, that he was feeling the same way I felt for so long, but I was so afraid that my life would become the hell it had been in my old school that I continued to ignore him.

Then, at recess one day, the meanest kid in the school, Chris, decided he had had enough of George. He vowed that he was going to beat up

George and anyone else who claimed to be his friend. A mob of kids formed and came after me. Chris led the way and cornered me near our school's swing sets. He grabbed me by my shirt and raised his fist over my head. A huge gathering of kids surrounded us, urging him to beat me up, chanting "Go, Chris, go!"

"You're Georgie's new little boyfriend, aren't you?" he yelled. The hot blast of his breath carried droplets of his spit into my face. In a complete betrayal of the only kid who was nice to me, I denied George's friendship.

"No, I'm not George's friend. I don't like him. He's stupid," I blurted out. Several kids snickered and mumbled under their breath. Chris stared at me for a few seconds and then threw me to the ground.

"Wimp. Where's George?" he demanded, standing over me. Someone pointed to George sitting alone on top of the monkey bars about thirty yards from where we were. He was watching me. Chris and his followers sprinted over to George and yanked him off the bars to the ground. Although the mob quickly encircled them, I could still see the two of them at the center of the crowd, looking at each other. George seemed stoic, staring straight through Chris. I heard the familiar chant of "Go, Chris, go!" and watched as his fists began slamming into George's head and body. His face bloodied and his nose broken, George crumpled to the ground and sobbed without even throwing a punch. The mob cheered with pleasure and darted off into the playground to avoid an approaching teacher.

Chris was suspended, and after a few days, George came back to school. I wanted to talk to him, to ask him how he was, to apologize for leaving him alone and for not trying to stop him from getting hurt. But I couldn't go near him. Filled with shame for denying George and angered by my own cowardice, I never spoke to him again.

Several months later, without telling any students, George transferred to another school. Once in a while, in those last weeks before he left, I caught him watching me as I sat with the rest of the kids in the cafeteria. He never yelled at me or expressed anger, disappointment, or even sadness. Instead he just looked at me.

In the years that followed, George's silent stare remained with me. It was there in eighth grade when I saw a gang of popular kids beat up a sixth-grader because, they said, he was "ugly and stupid." It was there my first year in high school, when I saw a group of older kids steal another freshman's clothes and throw them into the showers. It was there a year later, when I watched several seniors press a wad of chewing gum into the hair of a new girl on the bus. Each time that I witnessed another awkward, uncomfortable, scared kid being tormented, I thought of George, and gradually his haunting stare began to speak to me. No longer silent, it told me that every child who is picked on and taunted deserves better, that no one—no matter how big, strong, attractive or popular—has the right to abuse another person.

Finally, in my junior year when a loud-mouthed, pink-skinned bully named Donald began picking on two freshmen on the bus, I could no longer deny George. Donald was crumpling a large wad of paper and preparing to bounce it off the back of the head of one of the young students when I interrupted him.

"Leave them alone, Don," I said. By then I was six inches taller and, after two years of high-school wrestling, thirty pounds heavier than I had been in my freshman year. Though Donald was still two years older than me, he wasn't much bigger. He stopped what he was doing, squinted and stared at me.

"What's your problem, Paul?"

I felt the way I had many years earlier on the

playground when I watched the mob of kids begin to surround George.

"Just leave them alone. They aren't bothering you," I responded quietly.

"What's it to you?" he challenged. A glimpse of my own past, of rowing the bus, of being mocked for my clothes, my lisp, my glasses, and my absent father flashed in my mind.

"Just don't mess with them. That's all I am saying, Don." My fingertips were tingling. The bus was silent. He got up from his seat and leaned over me, and I rose from my seat to face him. For a minute, both of us just stood there, without a word, staring.

"I'm just playing with them, Paul," he said, chuckling. "You don't have to go psycho on me or anything." Then he shook his head, slapped me firmly on the chest with the back of his hand, and sat down. But he never threw that wad of paper. For the rest of the year, whenever I was on the bus, Don and the other troublemakers were noticeably quiet.

Although it has been years since my days on the playground and the school bus, George's look still haunts me. Today, I see it on the faces of a few scared kids at my sister's school—she is in fifth grade. Or once in a while I'll catch a glimpse of someone like George on the evening news, in a story about a child who brought a gun to school to stop the kids from picking on him, or in a feature about a teenager who killed herself because everyone teased her. In each school, in almost every classroom, there is a George with a stricken face, hoping that someone nearby will be strong enough to be kind—despite what the crowd says—and brave enough to stand up against people who attack, tease or hurt those who are vulnerable.

If asked about their behavior, I'm sure the bullies would say, "What's it to you? It's just a joke. It's nothing." But to George and me, and everyone else who has been humiliated or laughed at or spat on, it is everything. No one should have to row the bus.

## PREVIEW

All of us have suffered disappointments and moments when we have felt we've been treated unfairly. In this story, Marta Salinas writes about one such moment in her childhood in southern Texas. By focusing on an award that school authorities decided she should not receive, Marta shows us the pain of discrimination as well as the need for inner strength.

# THE SCHOLARSHIP JACKET

*Marta Salinas*

The small Texas school that I attended carried out a tradition every year during the eighth grade graduation: a beautiful gold and green jacket, the school colors, was awarded to the class valedictorian, the student who had maintained the highest grades for eight years. The scholarship jacket had a big gold S on the left front side, and the winner's name was written in gold letters on the pocket.

My oldest sister, Rosie, had won the jacket a few years back, and I fully expected to win also. I was fourteen and in the eighth grade. I had been a straight A student since the first grade, and the last year I had looked forward to owning that jacket. My father was a farm laborer who couldn't earn enough money to feed eight children, so when I was six I was given to my grandparents to raise. We couldn't participate in sports at school because there were registration fees, uniform costs, and trips out of town; so even though we were quite agile and athletic, there would never be a sports school jacket for us. This one, the scholarship jacket, was our only chance.

In May, close to graduation, spring fever struck, and no one paid any attention to class; instead we stared out the windows and at each other, wanting to speed up the last few weeks of school. I despaired every time I looked in the mirror. Pencil thin, not a curve anywhere, I was called "Beanpole" and "String Bean," and I knew that's what I looked like. A flat chest, no hips, and a brain, that's what I had. That really isn't much for a fourteen-year-old to work with,

I thought, as I absentmindedly wandered from my history class to the gym. Another hour of sweating during basketball and displaying my toothpick legs was coming up. Then I remembered my P.E. shorts were still in a bag under my desk where I'd forgotten them. I had to walk all the way back and get them. Coach Thompson was a real bear if anyone wasn't dressed for P.E. She had said I was a good forward and once she even tried to talk Grandma into letting me join the team. Grandma, of course, said no.

I was almost back at my classroom door when I heard angry voices and arguing. I stopped. I didn't mean to eavesdrop; I just hesitated, not knowing what to do. I needed those shorts and I was going to be late, but I didn't want to interrupt an argument between my teachers. I recognized the voices: Mr. Schmidt, my history teacher, and Mr. Boone, my math teacher. They seemed to be arguing about me. I couldn't believe it. I still remember the shock that rooted me flat against the wall as if I were trying to blend in with the graffiti written there.

"I refuse to do it! I don't care who her father is, her grades don't even begin to compare to Martha's. I won't lie or falsify records. Martha has a straight A plus average and you know it." That was Mr. Schmidt, and he sounded very angry. Mr. Boone's voice sounded calm and quiet.

"Look, Joann's father is not only on the Board, he owns the only store in town; we could say it was a close tie and—"

The pounding in my ears drowned out the rest of the words, only a word here and there filtered through. ". . . Martha is Mexican . . . resign . . . won't do it . . ." Mr. Schmidt came rushing out, and luckily for me went down the opposite way toward the auditorium, so he didn't see me. Shaking, I waited a few minutes and then went in and grabbed my bag and fled from the room. Mr. Boone looked up when I came in but didn't say anything. To this day I don't remember if I got in trouble in P.E. for being late or how I made it through the rest of the afternoon. I went home very sad and cried into my pillow that night so Grandmother wouldn't hear me. It seemed a cruel coincidence that I had overheard that conversation.

The next day when the principal called me into his office, I knew what it would be about. He looked uncomfortable and unhappy. I decided I wasn't going to make it any easier for him, so I looked him straight in the eye. He looked away and fidgeted with the papers on his desk.

"Martha," he said, "there's been a change in policy this year regarding the scholarship jacket. As you know, it has always been free." He cleared his throat and continued. "This year the Board decided to charge fifteen dollars—which still won't cover the complete cost of the jacket."

I stared at him in shock and a small sound of dismay escaped my throat. I hadn't expected this. He still avoided looking in my eyes.

"So if you are unable to pay the fifteen dollars for the jacket, it will be given to the next one in line."

Standing with all the dignity I could muster, I said, "I'll speak to my grandfather about it, sir, and let you know tomorrow." I cried on the walk home from the bus stop. The dirt road was a quarter of a mile from the highway, so by the time I got home, my eyes were red and puffy.

"Where's Grandpa?" I asked Grandma, looking down at the floor so she wouldn't ask me why I'd been crying. She was sewing on a quilt and didn't look up.

"I think he's out back working in the bean field."

I went outside and looked out at the fields. There he was. I could see him walking between the rows, his body bent over the little plants, hoe in hand. I walked slowly out to him, trying to think how I could best ask him for the money. There was a cool breeze blowing and a sweet smell of mesquite in the air, but I didn't appreciate it. I kicked at a dirt clod. I wanted that jacket so much. It was more than just being a valedictorian and giving a little thank-you speech for the jacket on graduation night. It represented eight years of hard work and expectation. I knew I had to be honest with Grandpa; it was my only chance. He saw me and looked up.

He waited for me to speak. I cleared my throat nervously and clasped my hands behind my back so he wouldn't see them shaking. "Grandpa, I have a big favor to ask you," I said in Spanish, the only language he knew. He still waited silently. I tried again. "Grandpa, this year the principal said the scholarship jacket is not going to be free. It's going to cost fifteen dollars and I have to take the money in tomorrow, otherwise it'll be given to someone else." The last words came out in an eager rush. Grandpa straightened up tiredly and leaned his chin on the hoe handle. He looked out over the field that was filled with the tiny green bean plants. I waited, desperately hoping he'd say I could have the money.

He turned to me and asked quietly, "What does a scholarship jacket mean?"

I answered quickly; maybe there was a chance. "It means you've earned it by having the highest grades for eight years and that's why they're giving it to you." Too late I realized the significance of my words. Grandpa knew that I understood it was not a matter of money. It wasn't that. He went back to hoeing the weeds that sprang up between the delicate little bean plants. It was a time-consuming job; sometimes the small shoots were right next to each other. Finally he spoke again.

"Then if you pay for it, Marta, it's not a scholarship jacket, is it? Tell your principal I will not pay the fifteen dollars."

I walked back to the house and locked myself in the bathroom for a long time. I was angry with Grandfather even though I knew he was right, and I was angry with the Board, whoever they were. Why did they have to change the rules just when it was my turn to win the jacket?

It was a very sad and withdrawn girl who dragged into the principal's office the next day. This time he did look me in the eyes.

"What did your grandfather say?"

I sat very straight in my chair.

"He said to tell you he won't pay the fifteen dollars."

The principal muttered something I couldn't understand under his breath, and walked over to the window. He stood looking out at something outside. He looked bigger than usual when he stood up; he was a tall, gaunt man with gray hair, and I watched the back of his head while I waited for him to speak.

"Why?" he finally asked. "Your grandfather has the money. Doesn't he own a small bean farm?"

I looked at him, forcing my eyes to stay dry. "He said if I had to pay for it, then it wouldn't be a scholarship jacket," I said and stood up to leave. "I guess you'll just have to give it to Joann." I hadn't meant to say that; it had just slipped out. I was almost to the door when he stopped me.

"Martha—wait."

I turned and looked at him, waiting. What did he want now? I could feel my heart pounding. Something bitter and vile tasting was coming up in my mouth; I was afraid I was going to be sick. I didn't need any sympathy speeches. He sighed loudly and went back to his big desk. He looked at me, biting his lip, as if thinking.

"Okay, damn it. We'll make an exception in your case. I'll tell the Board, you'll get your jacket."

I could hardly believe it. I spoke in a trembling rush. "Oh, thank you, sir!" Suddenly I felt great. I didn't know about adrenaline in those days, but I knew something was pumping through me, making me feel as tall as the sky. I wanted to yell, jump, run the mile, do something. I ran out so I could cry in the hall where there was no one to see me. At the end of the day, Mr. Schmidt winked at me and said, "I hear you're getting a scholarship jacket this year."

His face looked as happy and innocent as a baby's, but I knew better. Without answering I gave him a quick hug and ran to the bus. I cried on the walk home again, but this time because I was so happy. I couldn't wait to tell Grandpa and ran straight to the field. I joined him in the row where he was working and without saying anything I crouched down and started pulling up the weeds with my hands. Grandpa worked alongside me for a few minutes, but he didn't ask what had happened. After I had a little pile of weeds between the rows, I stood up and faced him.

"The principal said he's making an exception for me, Grandpa, and I'm getting the jacket after all. That's after I told him what you said."

Grandpa didn't say anything; he just gave me a pat on the shoulder and a smile. He pulled out the crumpled red handkerchief that he always carried in his back pocket and wiped the sweat off his forehead.

"Better go see if your grandmother needs any help with supper."

I gave him a big grin. He didn't fool me. I skipped and ran back to the house whistling some silly tune.

## PREVIEW

It is a sequence of events that occurs all too often—high-school kids gather for a party that quickly turns drunken and raucous. The party spills out into the roadways, and an evening of alcohol-fueled celebration turns into a nightmare of twisted metal, mangled bodies, and anguished survivors. As this article makes clear, the horror of such a night does not end with the funerals of those who died.

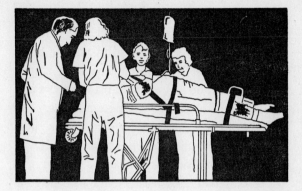

# A DRUNKEN RIDE,
# A TRAGIC AFTERMATH

*Theresa Conrad and
Christine M. Johnson*

When Tyson Baxter awoke after that drunken, tragic night—with a bloodied head, broken arm, and battered face—he knew that he had killed his friends.

"I knew everyone had died," Baxter, 18, recalled. "I knew it before anybody told me. Somehow, I knew."

Baxter was talking about the night of Friday, September 13, the night he and seven friends piled into his Chevrolet Blazer after a beer-drinking party. On Street Road in Upper Southampton, he lost control, rear-ended a car, and smashed into two telephone poles. The Blazer's cab top shattered, and the truck spun several times, ejecting all but one passenger.

Four young men were killed.

Tests would show that Baxter and the four youths who died were legally intoxicated.

Baxter says he thinks about his dead friends on many sleepless nights at the Abraxas Drug and Alcohol Rehabilitation Center near Pittsburgh, where, on December 20, he was sentenced to be held after being found delinquent on charges of vehicular homicide.

"I drove them where they wanted to go, and I was responsible for their lives," Baxter said recently from the center, where he is undergoing psychological treatment. "I had the keys in my hand, and I blew it."

The story of September 13 is a story about the kind of horrors that drinking and driving is spawning among high-school students almost everywhere, . . . about parents who lost their children in a flash and have filled the emptiness with hatred, . . . about a youth whose life is burdened with grief and guilt because he happened to be behind the wheel.

It is a story that the Baxter family and the dead boys' parents agreed to tell in the hope that it would inspire high-school students to remain sober during this week of graduation festivities—a week that customarily includes a ritual night of drunkenness.

It is a story of the times.

The evening of September 13 began in high spirits as Baxter, behind the wheel of his gold Blazer, picked up seven high-school chums for a drinking party for William Tennent High School students and graduates at the home of a classmate. Using false identification, according to police, the boys purchased one six-pack of beer each from a Warminster Township bar.

The unchaperoned party, attended by about fifty teenagers, ended about 10:30 p.m. when someone knocked over and broke a glass china cabinet. Baxter and his friends decided to head for a fast-food restaurant. As Baxter turned onto Street Road, he was trailed by a line of cars carrying other partygoers.

Baxter recalled that several passengers were swaying and rocking the high-suspension vehicle. Police were unable to determine the vehicle's exact speed, but, on the basis of the accounts of witnesses, they estimated it at fifty-five miles per hour—ten miles per hour over the limit.

"I thought I was in control," Baxter said. "I wasn't driving like a nut; I was just . . . driving. There was a bunch of noise, just a bunch of noise. The truck was really bouncing.

"I remember passing two [cars]. That's the last I remember. I remember a big flash, and that's it."

Killed in that flash were: Morris "Marty" Freedenberg, 16, who landed near a telephone pole about thirty feet from the truck, his face ripped from his skull; Robert Schweiss, 18, a Bucks County Community College student, whose internal organs were crushed when he hit the pavement about thirty feet from the truck; Brian Ball, 17, who landed near Schweiss, his six-foot-seven-inch frame stretched three inches when his spine was severed; and Christopher Avram, 17, a premedical student at Temple University, who landed near the curb about ten feet from the truck.

Michael Serratore, 18, was thrown fifteen feet from the truck and landed on the lawn of the CHI Institute with his right leg shattered. Baxter, who sailed about ten feet after crashing

through the windshield of the Blazer, lost consciousness after hitting the street near the center
lane. About five yards away, Paul Gee, Jr., 18,
lapsed into a coma from severe head injuries.

John Gahan, 17, the only passenger left in
the Blazer, suffered a broken ankle.

Brett Walker, 17, one of several Tennent
students who saw the carnage after the accident,
would recall later in a speech to fellow students:
"I ran over [to the scene]. These were the kids
I would go out with every weekend.

"My one friend [Freedenberg], I couldn't
even tell it was him except for his eyes. He had
real big, blue eyes. He was torn apart so bad. . . ."

Francis Schweiss was waiting up for his son,
Robert, when he received a telephone call from
his daughter, Lisa. She was already at
Warminster General Hospital.

"She said Robbie and his friends were in a
bad accident and Robbie was not here" at the
hospital, Schweiss said. "I got in my car with my
wife; we went to the scene of the accident."

There, police officers told Francis and
Frances Schweiss that several boys had been
killed and that the bodies, as well as survivors,
had been taken to Warminster General Hospital.

"My head was frying by then," Francis

Schweiss said. "I can't even describe it. I almost knew the worst was to be. I felt as though I were living a nightmare. I thought, 'I'll wake up. This just can't be.'"

In the emergency room, Francis Schweiss recalled, nurses and doctors were scrambling to aid the injured and identify the dead—a difficult task because some bodies were disfigured and because all the boys had been carrying fake driver's licenses.

A police officer from Upper Southampton was trying to question friends of the dead and injured—many of whom were sobbing and screaming—in an attempt to match clothing with identities.

When the phone rang in the Freedenberg home, Robert S. and his wife, Bobbi, had just gone upstairs to bed; their son Robert Jr. was downstairs watching a movie on television.

Bobbi Freedenberg and her son picked up the receiver at the same time. It was from Warminster General. . . . There had been a bad accident. . . . The family should get to the hospital quickly.

Outside the morgue about twenty minutes later, a deputy county coroner told Rob Jr., 22, that his brother was dead and severely disfigured; Rob decided to spare his parents addition-al grief by identifying the body himself.

Freedenberg was led into a cinderblock room containing large drawers resembling filing cabinets. In one of the drawers was his brother, Marty, identifiable only by his new high-top sneakers.

"It was kind of like being taken through a nightmare," Rob Jr. said. "That's something I think about every night before I go to sleep. That's hell. . . . That whole night is what hell is all about for me."

As was his custom, Morris Ball started calling the parents of his son's friends after Brian missed his 11:00 p.m. curfew.

The first call was to the Baxters' house, where the Baxters' sixteen-year-old daughter, Amber, told him about the accident.

At the hospital, Morris Ball demanded that doctors and nurses take him to his son. The hos-pital staff had been unable to identify Brian—until Ball told them that his son wore size 14 shoes.

Brian Ball was in the morgue. Lower left drawer.

"He was six foot seven, but after the acci-dent he measured six foot ten, because of what happened to him," Ball said. "He had a severed spinal cord at the neck. His buttocks were practically ripped off, but he was lying down and we couldn't see that. He was peaceful and asleep.

"He was my son and my baby. I just can't believe it sometimes. I still can't believe it. I still wait for him to come home."

Lynne Pancoast had just finished watching the 11:00 p.m. news and was curled up in her bed dozing with a book in her lap when the doorbell rang. She assumed that one of her sons had forgotten his key, and she went downstairs to let him in.

A police light was flashing through the window and reflecting against her living-room wall; Pancoast thought that there must be a fire in the neighborhood and that the police were evacuating homes.

Instead, police officers told her there had been a serious accident involving her son, Christopher Avram, and that she should go to the emergency room at Warminster General.

At the hospital she was taken to an empty room and told that her son was dead.

Patricia Baxter was asleep when a Warminster police officer came to the house and informed her that her son had been in an accident.

At the hospital, she could not immediately recognize her own son lying on a bed in the emergency room. His brown eyes were swollen shut, and his straight brown hair was matted with blood that had poured from a deep gash in his forehead.

While she was staring at his battered face, a police officer rushed into the room and pushed her onto the floor—protection against the hysterical father of a dead youth who was racing through the halls, proclaiming that he had a gun and shouting, "Where is she? I'm going to kill her. I'm going to kill him. I'm going to kill his mother."

The man, who did not have a gun, was subdued by a Warminster police officer and was not charged.

Amid the commotion, Robert Baxter, a Lower Southampton highway patrol officer, arrived at the hospital and found his wife and son.

"When he came into the room, he kept going like this," Patricia Baxter said, holding up four fingers. At first, she said, she did not understand that her husband was signaling that four boys had been killed in the accident.

After Tyson regained consciousness, his

father told him about the deaths.

"All I can remember is just tensing up and just saying something," Tyson Baxter said. "I can remember saying, 'I know.'

"I can remember going nuts."

In the days after the accident, as the dead were buried in services that Tyson Baxter was barred by the parents of the victims from attending, Baxter's parents waited for him to react to the tragedy and release his grief.

"In the hospital he was nonresponsive," Patricia Baxter said. "He was home for a month, and he was nonresponsive.

"We never used to do this, but we would be upstairs and listen to see if Ty responded when his friends came to visit," she said. "But the boy would be silent. That's the grief that I felt. The other kids showed a reaction. My son didn't."

Baxter said, however, that he felt grief from the first, that he would cry in the quiet darkness of his hospital room and, later, alone in the darkness of his bedroom. During the day, he said, he blocked his emotions.

"It was just at night. I thought about it all the time. It's still like that."

At his parents' urging, Baxter returned to school on September 30.

"I don't remember a thing," he said of his return. "I just remember walking around. I didn't say anything to anybody. It didn't really sink in."

Lynne Pancoast, the mother of Chris Avram, thought it was wrong for Baxter to be in school, and wrong that her other son, Joel, a junior at William Tennent, had to walk through the school halls and pass the boy who "killed his brother."

Morris Ball said he was appalled that Baxter "went to a football game while my son lay buried in a grave."

Some William Tennent students said they were uncertain about how they should treat Baxter. Several said they went out of their way to treat him normally, others said they tried to avoid him, and others declined to be interviewed on the subject.

The tragedy unified the senior class, according to the school principal, Kenneth Kastle. He said that after the accident, many students who were friends of the victims joined the school's Students Against Driving Drunk chapter.

Matthew Weintraub, 17, a basketball player who witnessed the bloody accident scene, wrote to President Reagan and detailed the grief among the student body. He said, however, that he experienced a catharsis after reading the let-

ter at a student assembly and, as a result, did not
mail it.

"And after we got over the initial shock of
the news, we felt as though we owed somebody
something," Weintraub wrote. "It could have
been us and maybe we could have stopped it,
and now it's too late. . . .

"We took these impressions with us as we
then visited our friends who had been lucky
enough to live. One of them was responsible for
the accident; he was the driver. He would forever
hold the deaths of four young men on his con-
science. Compared with our own feelings of guilt,
[we] could not begin to fathom this boy's emotions. He looked as if he had a heavy weight upon
his head and it would remain there forever."

About three weeks after the accident,
Senator H. Craig Lewis (D., Bucks) launched a
series of public forums to formulate bills target-
ing underage drinking. Proposals developed
through the meetings include outlawing alcohol
ads on radio and television, requiring police to
notify parents of underage drinkers, and creat-
ing a tamperproof driver's license.

The parents of players on William Tennent's
1985–1986 boys' basketball team, which lost
Ball and Baxter because of the accident, formed
the Caring Parents of William Tennent High

School Students to help dissuade students from drinking.

Several William Tennent students, interviewed on the condition that their names not be published, said that, because of the accident, they would not drive after drinking during senior week, which will be held in Wildwood, New Jersey, after graduation June 13.

But they scoffed at the suggestion that they curtail their drinking during the celebrations.

"We just walk [after driving to Wildwood]," said one youth. "Stagger is more like it."

"What else are we going to do, go out roller skating?" an eighteen-year-old student asked.

"You telling us we're not going to drink?" one boy asked. "We're going to drink very heavily. I want to come home retarded. That's senior week. I'm going to drink every day. Everybody's going to drink every day."

Tyson Baxter sat at the front table of the Bucks County courtroom on December 20, his arm in a sling, his head lowered and his eyes dry. He faced twenty counts of vehicular homicide, four counts of involuntary manslaughter, and two counts of driving under the influence of alcohol.

Patricia Ball said she told the closed hearing that "it was Tyson Baxter who killed our son. He used the car as a weapon. We know he killed our children as if it were a gun. He killed our son."

"I really could have felt justice [was served] if Tyson Baxter was the only one who died in that car," she said in an interview, "because he didn't take care of our boys."

Police officers testified before Bucks County President Judge Isaac S. Garb that tests revealed that the blood-alcohol levels of Baxter and the four dead boys were above the 0.10 percent limit used in Pennsylvania to establish intoxication.

Baxter's blood-alcohol level was 0.14 percent, Ball's 0.19 percent, Schweiss's 0.11 percent, Avram's 0.12 percent, and Freedenberg's 0.38 percent. Baxter's level indicated that he had had eight or nine drinks—enough to cause abnormal bodily functions such as exaggerated gestures and to impair his mental faculties, according to the police report.

After the case was presented, Garb invited family members of the dead teens to speak.

In a nine-page statement, Bobbi Freedenberg urged Garb to render a decision that would "punish, rehabilitate, and deter others from this act."

The parents asked Garb to give Baxter the maximum sentence, to prohibit him from graduating, and to incarcerate him before Christmas day. (Although he will not attend formal ceremonies, Baxter will receive a diploma from William Tennent this week.)

After hearing from the parents, Garb called Baxter to the stand.

"I just said that all I could say was, 'I'm sorry; I know I'm totally responsible for what happened,'" Baxter recalled. "It wasn't long, but it was to the point."

Garb found Baxter delinquent and sentenced him to a stay at Abraxas Rehabilitation Center—for an unspecified period beginning December 23—and community service upon his return. Baxter's driver's license was suspended by the judge for an unspecified period, and he was placed under Garb's jurisdiction until age 21.

Baxter is one of fifty-two Pennsylvania youths found responsible for fatal drunken-driving accidents in the state in 1985.

Reflecting on the hearing, Morris Ball said there was no legal punishment that would have satisfied his longings.

"They can't bring my son back," he said, "and they can't kill Tyson Baxter."

Grief has forged friendships among the dead boys' parents, each of whom blames Tyson Baxter for their son's death. Every month they meet at each other's homes, but they seldom talk about the accident.

Several have joined support groups to help them deal with their losses. Some said they feel comfortable only with other parents whose children are dead.

Bobbi Freedenberg said her attitude had worsened with the passage of time. "It seems as if it just gets harder," she said. "It seems to get worse."

Freedenberg, Schweiss, and Pancoast said they talk publicly about their sons' deaths in hopes that the experience will help deter other teenagers from drunken driving.

Schweiss speaks each month to the Warminster Youth Aid Panel—a group of teenagers who, through drug use, alcohol abuse, or minor offenses, have run afoul of the law.

"When I talk to the teens, I bring a picture of Robbie and pass it along to everyone," Schweiss said, wiping the tears from his cheeks. "I say, 'He was with us last year.' I get emotional and I cry. . . .

"But I know that my son helps me. I firmly believe that every time I speak, he's right on my shoulder."

When Pancoast speaks to a group of area high-school students, she drapes her son's football jersey over the podium and displays his graduation picture.

"Every time I speak to a group, I make them go through the whole thing vicariously," Pancoast said. "It's helpful to get out and talk to kids. It sort of helps keep Chris alive. . . . When you talk, you don't think."

At Abraxas, Baxter attended high-school classes until Friday. He is one of three youths there who supervise fellow residents, who keep track of residents' whereabouts, attendance at programs, and adherence to the center's rules and regulations.

Established in Pittsburgh in 1973, the Abraxas Foundation provides an alternative to imprisonment for offenders between sixteen and twenty-five years old whose drug and alcohol use has led them to commit crimes.

Licensed and partially subsidized by the Pennsylvania Department of Health, the program includes work experience, high-school education, and prevocational training. Counselors conduct individual therapy sessions, and the residents engage in peer-group confrontational therapy sessions.

Baxter said his personality had changed from an "egotistical, arrogant" teenager to someone who is "mellow" and mature.

"I don't have quite the chip on my shoulder. I don't really have a right to be cocky anymore," he said.

Baxter said not a day went by that he didn't remember his dead friends.

"I don't get sad. I just get thinking about them," he said. "Pictures pop into my mind. A tree or something reminds me of the time. . . . Sometimes I laugh. . . . Then I go to my room and reevaluate it like a nut," he said.

Baxter said his deepest longing was to stand beside the graves of his four friends.

More than anything, Baxter said, he wants to say good-bye.

"I just feel it's something I have to do, . . . just to talk," Baxter said, averting his eyes to hide welling tears. "Deep down I think I'll be hit with it when I see the graves. I know they're gone, but they're not gone."

## PREVIEW

When Lupe Quintanilla was told "You can't learn," she accepted those humiliating words and left formal education behind her. But when her children were told the same thing, a fire was lit in Lupe's soul. Determined to help her children succeed, Lupe discovered abilities within herself she had never dreamed existed.

# THE PROFESSOR IS A DROPOUT

*Beth Johnson*

Guadalupe Quintanilla is an assistant professor at the University of Houston. She is president of her own communications company. She trains law enforcement officers all over the country. She was nominated to serve as the U.S. Attorney General. She's been a representative to the United Nations.

That's a pretty impressive string of accomplishments. It's all the more impressive when you consider this: "Lupe" Quintanilla is a first-grade dropout. Her school records state that she is retarded, that her IQ is so low she can't learn much of anything.

How did Lupe Quintanilla, "retarded" non-learner, become Dr. Quintanilla, respected educator? Her remarkable journey began in the town of Nogales, Mexico, just below the Arizona border. That's where Lupe first lived with her grandparents. (Her parents had divorced.) Then an uncle who had just finished medical school made her grandparents a generous offer. If they wanted to live with him, he would support the family as he began his medical practice.

Lupe, her grandparents, and her uncle all moved hundreds of miles to a town in southern Mexico that didn't even have paved roads, let alone any schools. There, Lupe grew up helping her grandfather run his little pharmacy and her grandmother keep house. She remembers the time happily. "My grandparents were wonderful," she said. "Oh, my grandfather was stern, authoritarian, as Mexican culture demanded, but they were also very kind to me." When the chores were done, her grandfather taught Lupe to read and write Spanish and do basic arithmetic.

When Lupe was 12, her grandfather became blind. The family left Mexico and went to Brownsville, Texas, with the hope that doctors there could restore his sight. Once they arrived in Brownsville, Lupe was enrolled in school. Although she understood no English, she was given an IQ test in that language. Not surprisingly, she didn't do very well.

Lupe even remembers her score. "I scored a sixty-four, which classified me as seriously retarded, not even teachable," she said. "I was put into first grade with a class of six-year-olds. My duties were to take the little kids to the bathroom and to cut out pictures." The classroom activities were a total mystery to Lupe— they were all conducted in English. And she was humiliated by the other children, who teased her for being "so much older and so much dumber" than they were.

After four months in first grade, an incident occurred that Lupe still does not fully understand. As she stood in the doorway of the classroom waiting to escort a little girl to the bathroom, a man approached her. He asked her, in Spanish, how to find the principal's office. Lupe was delighted. "Finally someone in this school had spoken to me with words I could understand, in the language of my soul, the language of my grandmother," she said. Eagerly, she answered his question in Spanish. Instantly her teacher swooped down on her, grabbing her arm and scolding her. She pulled Lupe along to the principal's office. There, the teacher and the principal both shouted at her, obviously very angry. Lupe was frightened and embarrassed, but also bewildered. She didn't understand a word they were saying.

"Why were they so angry? I don't know," said Lupe. "Was it because I spoke Spanish at school? Or that I spoke to the man at all? I really don't know. All I know is how humiliated I was."

When she got home that day, she cried miserably, begging her grandfather not to make her return to school. Finally he agreed.

From that time on, Lupe stayed at home, serving as her blind grandfather's "eyes." She was a fluent reader in Spanish, and the older man loved to have her read newspapers, poetry, and novels aloud to him for hours.

Lupe's own love of reading flourished during these years. Her vocabulary was enriched and her imagination fired by the novels she read—novels which she learned later were classics of Spanish literature. She read *Don Quixote*, the famous story of the noble, impractical knight who fought against windmills. She read thrilling accounts of the Mexican revolution. She read *La Prensa,* the local Spanish-language paper, and *Selecciones,* the Spanish-language version of *Reader's Digest.*

When she was just 16, Lupe married a young Mexican-American dental technician. Within five years, she had given birth to her three children, Victor, Mario, and Martha. Lupe's grandparents lived with the young family. Lupe was quite happy with her life. "I cooked, sewed, cleaned, and cared for everybody," she said. "I listened to my grandmother when she told me what made a good wife. In the morning I would actually put on my husband's shoes and tie the laces—anything to make his life easier. Living with my grandparents for so long, I was one generation behind in my ideas of what a woman could do and be."

Lupe's contentment ended when her children started school. When they brought home their report cards, she struggled to understand them. She could read enough English to know that what they said was not good. Her children had been put into a group called "Yellow Birds." It was a group for slow learners.

At night in bed, Lupe cried and blamed herself. It was obvious—not only was she retarded, but her children had taken after her. Now they, too, would never be able to learn like other children.

But in time, a thought began to break through Lupe's despair: Her children didn't seem like slow learners to her. At home, they learned everything she taught them, quickly and easily. She read to them constantly, from the books that she herself had loved as a child. *Aesop's Fables* and stories from *1,001 Arabian Nights* were family favorites. The children filled the house with the sounds of the songs, prayers, games, and rhymes they had learned from their parents and grandparents. They were smart children, eager to learn. They learned quickly—in Spanish.

A radical idea began to form in Lupe's mind. Maybe the school was wrong about her children. And if the school system could be wrong about her children—maybe it had been wrong about her, too.

Lupe visited her children's school, a daring action for her. "Many Hispanic parents would not dream of going to the classroom," she said. "In Hispanic culture, the teacher is regarded as a third parent, as an ultimate authority. To question her would seem most disrespectful, as though you were saying that she didn't know her job." That was one reason Lupe's grandparents had not interfered when Lupe was classified as retarded. "Anglo teachers often misunderstand Hispanic parents, believing that they aren't concerned about their children's education because they don't come visit the schools," Lupe said. "It's not a lack of concern at all. It's a mark of respect for the teacher's authority."

At her children's school, Lupe spoke to three different teachers. Two of them told her the same thing: "Your children are just slow. Sorry, but they can't learn." A third offered a glimmer of hope. He said, "They don't know how to function in English. It's possible that if you spoke English at home they would be able to do better."

Lupe pounced on that idea. "Where can I learn English?" she asked. The teacher shrugged. At that time there were no local English-language programs for adults. Finally he suggested that Lupe visit the local high school. Maybe she would be permitted to sit in the back of a classroom and pick up some English that way.

Lupe made an appointment with a counselor at the high school. But when the two women met, the counselor shook her head. "Your test scores show that you are retarded," she told

Lupe. "You'd just be taking space in the classroom away from someone who could learn."

Lupe's next stop was the hospital where she had served for years as a volunteer. Could she sit in on some of the nursing classes held there? No, she was told, not without a diploma. Still undeterred, she went on to Texas Southmost College in Brownsville. Could she sit in on a class? No; no high-school diploma. Finally she went to the telephone company, where she knew operators were being trained. Could she listen in on the classes? No, only high-school graduates were permitted.

That day, leaving the telephone company, Lupe felt she had hit bottom. She had been terrified in the first place to try to find an English class. Meeting with rejection after rejection nearly destroyed what little self-confidence she had. She walked home in the rain, crying. "I felt like a big barrier had fallen across my path," she said. "I couldn't go over it; I couldn't go under it; I couldn't go around it."

But the next day Lupe woke with fresh determination. "I was motivated by love of my kids," she said. "I was not going to quit." She got up; made breakfast for her kids, husband, and grandparents; saw her children and husband off for the day; and started out again. "I remember walking to the bus stop, past a dog that always scared me to death, and heading back to the college. The lady I spoke to said, 'I told you, we can't do anything for you without a high-school degree.' But as I left the building, I went up to the first Spanish-speaking student I saw. His name was Gabito. I said, 'Who really makes the decisions around here?' He said, 'The registrar.'" Since she hadn't had any luck in the office building, Lupe decided to take a more direct approach. She asked Gabito to point out the registrar's car in the parking lot. For the next two hours she waited beside it until its owner showed up.

Impressed by Lupe's persistence, the registrar listened to her story. But instead of giving her permission to sit in on a class and learn more English, he insisted that she sign up for a full college load. Before she knew it, she was enrolled in four classes: Basic Math, Basic English, Psychology, and Typing. The registrar's parting words to her were "Don't come back if you don't make it through."

With that "encouragement," Lupe began a semester that was part nightmare, part dream come true. Every day she got her husband and children off to school, took the bus to campus, came home to make lunch for her husband and grandparents, went back to campus, and was home in time to greet Victor, Mario, and Martha when they got home from school. In the evenings she cooked, cleaned, did laundry, and got the children to bed. Then she would study, often until three in the morning.

"Sometimes in class I would feel sick with the stress of it," she said. "I'd go to the bathroom and talk to myself in the mirror. Sometimes I'd say, 'What are you doing here? Why don't you go home and watch *I Love Lucy*?'"

But she didn't go home. Instead, she studied furiously, using her Spanish-English dictionary, constantly making lists of new words she wanted to understand. "I still do that today," she said. "When I come across a word I don't know, I write it down, look it up, and write sentences using it until I own that word."

Although so much of the language and subject matter was new to Lupe, one part of the college experience was not. That was the key skill of reading, a skill Lupe possessed. As she struggled with English, she found the reading speed, comprehension, and vocabulary that she had developed in Spanish carrying over into her new language. "Reading," she said, "reading was the vehicle. Although I didn't know it at the time, when I was a girl learning to love to read, I was laying the foundation for academic success."

She gives credit, too, to her Hispanic fellow students. "At first, they didn't know what to make of me. They were eighteen years old, and at that time it was very unfashionable for an older person to be in college. But once they decided I wasn't a 'plant' from the administration, they were my greatest help." The younger students spent hours helping Lupe, explaining unfamiliar words and terms, coaching her, and answering her questions.

That first semester passed in a fog of exhaustion. Many mornings, Lupe doubted she could get out of bed, much less care for her family and tackle her classes. But when she thought of her children and what was at stake for them, she forced herself on. She remembers well what those days were like. "Just a day at a time. That was all I could think about. I could make myself get up one more day, study one more day, cook and clean one more day. And those days eventually turned into a semester."

To her own amazement perhaps as much as anyone's, Lupe discovered that she was far from retarded. Although she sweated blood over many assignments, she completed them. She turned them in on time. And, remarkably, she made the dean's list her very first semester.

After that, there was no stopping Lupe Quintanilla. She soon realized that the associate's degree offered by Texas Southmost College would not satisfy her. Continuing her Monday, Wednesday, and Friday schedule at Southmost, she enrolled for Tuesday and Thursday courses at Pan American University, a school 140 miles from Brownsville. Within three years, she had earned both her junior-college degree and a bachelor's degree in biology. She then won a fellowship that took her to graduate school at the University of Houston, where she earned a master's degree in Spanish literature. When she graduated, the university offered her a job as director of the Mexican-American studies program. While in that position, she earned a doctoral degree in education.

How did she do it all? Lupe herself isn't sure. "I hardly know. When I think back to those years, it seems like a life that someone else lived." It was a rich and exciting but also very challenging period for Lupe and her family. On the one hand, Lupe was motivated by the desire to set an example for her children, to prove to them that they could succeed in the English-speaking academic world. On the other hand, she worried about neglecting her family. She tried hard to attend important activities, such as parents' meetings at school and her children's sporting events. But things didn't always work out. Lupe still remembers attending a baseball game that her older son, Victor, was playing in. When Victor came to bat, he hit a home run. But as the crowd cheered and Victor glanced proudly over at his mother in the stands, he saw she was studying a textbook. "I hadn't seen the home run," Lupe admitted. "That sort of thing was hard for everyone to take."

Although Lupe worried that her children would resent her busy schedule, she also saw her success reflected in them as they blossomed in school. She forced herself to speak English at home, and their language skills improved quickly. She read to them in English instead of Spanish—gulping down her pride as their pronunciation became better than hers and they began correcting her. (Once the children were in high school and fluent in English, Lupe switched back to Spanish at home, so that the children would be fully comfortable in both languages.) "I saw the change in them almost immediately," she said. "After I helped them with their homework, they would see me pulling out my own books and going to work. In the morning, I would show them the papers I had written. As I gained confidence, so did they." By the next year, the children had been promoted out of the Yellow Birds.

Even though Victor, Mario, and Martha all did well academically, Lupe realized she could not assume that they would face no more obstacles in school. When Mario was in high school, for instance, he wanted to sign up for a debate class. Instead, he was assigned to woodworking. She visited the school to ask why. Mario's teacher told her, "He's good with his hands. He'll be a great carpenter, and that's a good thing for a Mexican to be." Controlling her temper, Lupe responded, "I'm glad you think he's good with his hands. He'll be a great physician someday, and he is going to be in the debate class."

Today, Lupe Quintanilla teaches at the University of Houston, where she has developed several dozen courses concerning Hispanic literature and culture. Her cross-cultural training for law enforcement officers, which helps bring police and firefighters and local Hispanic communities closer together, is renowned throughout the country. Former President Ronald Reagan named her to a national board that keeps the White House informed of new programs in law enforcement. She has received numerous awards for teaching excellence, and there is even a scholarship named in her honor. Her name appears in the Hispanic Hall of Fame, and she has been co-chair of the White House Commission on Hispanic Education.

The love of reading that her grandfather instilled in Lupe is still alive. She thinks of him every year when she introduces to her students one of his favorite poets, Amado Nervo. She requires them to memorize these lines from one of Nervo's poems: "When I got to the end of my long journey in life, I realized that I was the architect of my own destiny." Of these lines, Lupe says, "That is something that I deeply believe, and I want my students to learn it before the end of their long journey. We create our own destiny."

Her love of reading and learning has helped Lupe create a distinguished destiny. But none of the honors she has received means more to her than the success of her own children, the reason she made that frightening journey to seek classes in English years ago. Today Mario is a physician. Victor and Martha are lawyers, both having earned doctor of law degrees. And so today, Lupe likes to say, "When someone calls the house and asks for 'Dr. Quintanilla,' I have to ask, 'Which one?' There are four of us—one retarded and three slow learners."

## PREVIEW

If you suspect that you are now as "smart" as you'll ever be, then read the following selection. Taken from the book *Think Big*, it is about Dr. Ben Carson, who was sure he was "the dumbest kid in the class" when he was in fifth grade. Carson tells how he turned his life totally around from what was a sure path of failure. Today he is a famous neurosurgeon at the Johns Hopkins University Children's Center in Baltimore, Maryland.

# DO IT BETTER!

*Ben Carson, M.D.,*
*with Cecil Murphey*

"Benjamin, is this your report card?" my
mother asked as she picked up the folded white
card from the table.

"Uh, yeah," I said, trying to sound casual.
Too ashamed to hand it to her, I had dropped it
on the table, hoping that she wouldn't notice
until after I went to bed.

It was the first report card I had received from Higgins Elementary School since we had moved back from Boston to Detroit, only a few months earlier.

I had been in the fifth grade not even two weeks before everyone considered me the dumbest kid in the class and frequently made jokes about me. Before long I too began to feel as though I really was the most stupid kid in fifth grade. Despite Mother's frequently saying, "You're smart, Bennie. You can do anything you want to do," I did not believe her.

No one else in school thought I was smart, either.

Now, as Mother examined my report card, she asked, "What's this grade in reading?" (Her tone of voice told me that I was in trouble.) Although I was embarrassed, I did not think too much about it. Mother knew that I wasn't doing well in math, but she did not know I was doing so poorly in every subject.

While she slowly read my report card, reading everything one word at a time, I hurried into my room and started to get ready for bed. A few minutes later, Mother came into my bedroom.

"Benjamin," she said, "are these your grades?" She held the card in front of me as if I hadn't seen it before.

"Oh, yeah, but you know, it doesn't mean much."

"No, that's not true, Bennie. It means a lot."

"Just a report card."

"But it's more than that."

Knowing I was in for it now, I prepared to listen, yet I was not all that interested. I did not like school very much and there was no reason why I should. Inasmuch as I was the dumbest kid in the class, what did I have to look forward to? The others laughed at me and made jokes about me every day.

"Education is the only way you're ever going to escape poverty," she said. "It's the only way you're ever going to get ahead in life and be successful. Do you understand that?"

"Yes, Mother," I mumbled.

"If you keep on getting these kinds of grades you're going to spend the rest of your life on skid row, or at best sweeping floors in a factory. That's not the kind of life that I want for you. That's not the kind of life that God wants for you."

I hung my head, genuinely ashamed. My mother had been raising me and my older brother, Curtis, by herself. Having only a third-grade education herself, she knew the value of what she did not have. Daily she drummed into Curtis and me that we had to do our best in school.

"You're just not living up to your potential," she said. "I've got two mighty smart boys and I know they can do better."

I had done my best—at least I had when I first started at Higgins Elementary School. How could I do much when I did not understand anything going on in our class?

In Boston we had attended a parochial school, but I hadn't learned much because of a teacher who seemed more interested in talking to another female teacher than in teaching us. Possibly, this teacher was not solely to blame—perhaps I wasn't emotionally able to learn much. My parents had separated just before we went to Boston, when I was eight years old. I loved both my mother and father and went through considerable trauma over their separating. For months afterward, I kept thinking that my parents would get back together, that my daddy would come home again the way he used to, and that we could be the same old family again—but he never came back. Consequently, we moved to Boston and lived with Aunt Jean and Uncle William Avery in a tenement building for two years until Mother had saved enough money to bring us back to Detroit.

Mother kept shaking the report card at me as she sat on the side of my bed. "You have to work harder. You have to use that good brain that God gave you, Bennie. Do you understand that?"

"Yes, Mother." Each time she paused, I would dutifully say those words.

"I work among rich people, people who are

educated," she said. "I watch how they act, and I know they can do anything they want to do. And so can you." She put her arm on my shoulder. "Bennie, you can do anything they can do—only you can do it better!"

Mother had said those words before. Often. At the time, they did not mean much to me. Why should they? I really believed that I was the dumbest kid in fifth grade, but of course, I never told her that.

"I just don't know what to do about you boys," she said. "I'm going to talk to God about you and Curtis." She paused, stared into space, then said (more to herself than to me), "I need the Lord's guidance on what to do. You just can't bring in any more report cards like this."

As far as I was concerned, the report card matter was over.

The next day was like the previous ones— just another bad day in school, another day of being laughed at because I did not get a single problem right in arithmetic and couldn't get any words right on the spelling test. As soon as I came home from school, I changed into play clothes and ran outside. Most of the boys my age played softball, or the game I liked best, "Tip the Top."

We played Tip the Top by placing a bottle cap on one of the sidewalk cracks. Then taking a ball—any kind that bounced—we'd stand on a line and take turns throwing the ball at the bottle top, trying to flip it over. Whoever succeeded got two points. If anyone actually moved the cap more than a few inches, he won five points. Ten points came if he flipped it into the air and it landed on the other side.

When it grew dark or we got tired, Curtis and I would finally go inside and watch TV. The set stayed on until we went to bed. Because Mother worked long hours, she was never home until just before we went to bed. Sometimes I would awaken when I heard her unlocking the door.

Two evenings after the incident with the report card, Mother came home about an hour before our bedtime. Curtis and I were sprawled out, watching TV. She walked across the room, snapped off the set, and faced both of us. "Boys," she said, "you're wasting too much of your time in front of that television. You don't get an education from staring at television all the time."

Before either of us could make a protest, she told us that she had been praying for wisdom. "The Lord's told me what to do," she said. "So from now on, you will not watch television, except for two preselected programs each week."

"Just two programs?" I could hardly believe she would say such a terrible thing. "That's not—"

"And only after you've done your homework. Furthermore, you don't play outside after school, either, until you've done all your homework."

"Everybody else plays outside right after school," I said, unable to think of anything except how bad it would be if I couldn't play with my friends. "I won't have any friends if I stay in the house all the time—"

"That may be," Mother said, "but everybody else is not going to be as successful as you are—"

"But, Mother—"

"This is what we're going to do. I asked God for wisdom, and this is the answer I got."

I tried to offer several other arguments, but Mother was firm. I glanced at Curtis, expecting him to speak up, but he did not say anything. He lay on the floor, staring at his feet.

"Don't worry about everybody else. The whole world is full of 'everybody else,' you know that? But only a few make a significant achievement."

The loss of TV and play time was bad enough. I got up off the floor, feeling as if everything was against me. Mother wasn't going to let me play with my friends, and there would be no more television—almost none, anyway. She was stopping me from having any fun in life.

"And that isn't all," she said. "Come back, Bennie."

I turned around, wondering what else there could be.

"In addition," she said, "to doing your homework, you have to read two books from the library each week. Every single week."

"Two books? Two?" Even though I was in fifth grade, I had never read a whole book in my life.

"Yes, two. When you finish reading them, you must write me a book report just like you do at school. You're not living up to your potential, so I'm going to see that you do."

Usually Curtis, who was two years older, was the more rebellious. But this time he seemed to grasp the wisdom of what Mother said. He did not say one word.

She stared at Curtis. "You understand?"

He nodded.

"Bennie, is it clear?"

"Yes, Mother." I agreed to do what Mother told me—it wouldn't have occurred to me not to obey—but I did not like it. Mother was being unfair and demanding more of us than other parents did.

The following day was Thursday. After school, Curtis and I walked to the local branch of the library. I did not like it much, but then I had not spent that much time in any library.

We both wandered around a little in the children's section, not having any idea about how to select books or which books we wanted to check out.

The librarian came over to us and asked if she could help. We explained that both of us wanted to check out two books.

"What kind of books would you like to read?" the librarian asked.

"Animals," I said after thinking about it. "Something about animals."

"I'm sure we have several that you'd like." She led me over to a section of books. She left me and guided Curtis to another section of the room. I flipped through the row of books until I found two that looked easy enough for me to read. One of them, Chip, the Dam Builder—about a beaver—was the first one I had ever checked out. As soon as I got home, I started to read it. It was the first book I ever read all the way through even though it took me two nights. Reluctantly I admitted afterward to Mother that I really had liked reading about Chip.

Within a month I could find my way around the children's section like someone who had gone there all his life. By then the library staff knew Curtis and me and the kind of books we chose. They often made suggestions. "Here's a delightful book about a squirrel," I remember one of them telling me.

As she told me part of the story, I tried to appear indifferent, but as soon as she handed it to me, I opened the book and started to read.

Best of all, we became favorites of the librarians. When new books came in that they thought either of us would enjoy, they held them for us. Soon I became fascinated as I realized that the library had so many books—and about so many different subjects.

After the book about the beaver, I chose others about animals—all types of animals. I read every animal story I could get my hands on. I read books about wolves, wild dogs, several about squirrels, and a variety of animals that lived in other countries. Once I had gone through the animal books, I started reading about plants, then minerals, and finally rocks.

My reading books about rocks was the first time the information ever became practical to me. We lived near the railroad tracks, and when Curtis and I took the route to school that crossed by the tracks, I began paying attention to the crushed rock that I noticed between the ties.

As I continued to read more about rocks, I would walk along the tracks, searching for different kinds of stones, and then see if I could identify them.

Often I would take a book with me to make sure that I had labeled each stone correctly.

"Agate," I said as I threw the stone. Curtis got tired of my picking up stones and identifying them, but I did not care because I kept finding new stones all the time. Soon it became my favorite game to walk along the tracks and identify the varieties of stones. Although I did not realize it, within a very short period of time, I was actually becoming an expert on rocks.

Two things happened in the second half of fifth grade that convinced me of the importance of reading books.

First, our teacher, Mrs. Williamson, had a spelling bee every Friday afternoon. We'd go through all the words we'd had so far that year. Sometimes she also called out words that we were supposed to have learned in fourth grade. Without fail, I always went down on the first word.

One Friday, though, Bobby Farmer, whom everyone acknowledged as the smartest kid in our class, had to spell "agriculture" as his final word. As soon as the teacher pronounced his word, I thought, I can spell that word. Just the day before, I had learned it from reading one of my library books. I spelled it under my breath, and it was just the way Bobby spelled it.

If I can spell "agriculture," I'll bet I can learn to spell any other word in the world. I'll bet I can learn to spell better than Bobby Farmer.

Just that single word, "agri-culture," was enough to give me hope.

The following week, a second thing happened that forever changed my life. When Mr. Jaeck, the science teacher, was teaching us about volcanoes, he held up an object that looked like a piece of black, glass-like rock. "Does anybody know what this is? What does it have to do with volcanoes?"

Immediately, because of my reading, I recognized the stone. I waited, but none of my classmates raised their hands. I thought, This is strange. Not even the smart kids are raising their hands. I raised my hand.

"Yes, Benjamin," he said.

I heard snickers around me. The other kids probably thought it was a joke, or that I was going to say something stupid.

"Obsidian," I said.

"That's right!" He tried not to look startled, but it was obvious he hadn't expected me to give the correct answer.

"That's obsidian," I said, "and it's formed by the supercooling of lava when it hits the water." Once I had their attention and realized I knew information no other student had learned, I began to tell them everything I knew about the subject of obsidian, lava, lava flow, supercooling, and compacting of the elements.

When I finally paused, a voice behind me whispered, "Is that Bennie Carson?"

"You're absolutely correct," Mr. Jaeck said and he smiled at me. If he had announced that I'd won a million-dollar lottery, I couldn't have been more pleased and excited.

"Benjamin, that's absolutely, absolutely right," he repeated with enthusiasm in his voice. He turned to the others and said, "That is wonderful! Class, this is a tremendous piece of information Benjamin has just given us. I'm very proud to hear him say this."

For a few moments, I tasted the thrill of achievement. I recall thinking, Wow, look at them. They're all looking at me with admiration. Me, the dummy! The one everybody thinks is stupid. They're looking at me to see if this is really me speaking.

Maybe, though, it was I who was the most astonished one in the class. Although I had been reading two books a week because Mother told me to, I had not realized how much knowledge I was accumulating. True, I had learned to enjoy reading, but until then I hadn't realized how it connected with my schoolwork. That day—for the first time—I realized that Mother had been right. Reading is the way out of ignorance, and the road to achievement. I did not have to be the class dummy anymore.

For the next few days, I felt like a hero at school. The jokes about me stopped. The kids started to listen to me. I'm starting to have fun with this stuff.

As my grades improved in every subject, I asked myself, "Ben, is there any reason you can't be the smartest kid in the class? If you can learn about obsidian, you can learn about social studies and geography and math and science and everything."

That single moment of triumph pushed me to want to read more. From then on, it was as though I could not read enough books. Whenever anyone looked for me after school, they could usually find me in my bedroom—curled up, reading a library book—for a long time, the only thing I wanted to do. I had stopped caring about the TV programs I was missing; I no longer cared about playing Tip the Top or baseball anymore. I just wanted to read.

In a year and a half—by the middle of sixth grade—I had moved to the top of the class.

## PREVIEW

A small, furry body lies on the pavement. It's a daily reality for most of us, living as we do in a world where the automobile rules the road. But in this case, something moved the author to stop and investigate. What he found reminded him that the chance to save a life doesn't come along every day.

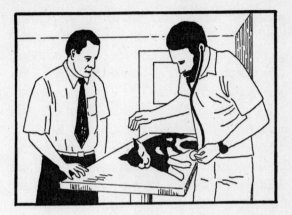

# LIFE OVER DEATH

*Bill Broderick*

My reaction was as it always is when I see an animal lying in the roadway. My heart sank. And a lump formed in my throat at the thought of a life unfulfilled. I then resolved to move him off the road, to ensure that one of God's creations did not become a permanent part of the pavement. Some might ask what difference it makes. If it's already dead, why not just leave it there? My answer is that I believe in death with dignity, for people and for animals alike.

So I pulled my car over to the side of the

road and walked back to where the cat lay motionless. Two cars passed over him, managing to avoid running him over. With no other cars in sight, I made my way to the lifeless form just as a jogger went by. The jogger grimaced at the sight of the immobile cat, blood dripping from his mouth. "How'd it happen?" he asked. I replied that I didn't know; he probably got hit by some careless driver. I just wanted to get him off the road. I reached down for the cat and got the surprise of my life. The little creature lifted his head ever so slightly and uttered a pitiful, unforgettable little "meow." He was still alive.

What was I going to do now? I was already late for work. All I had intended to do was move the cat off the road. I didn't need this. But I knew I had no choice. I sighed deeply, then reached down and carefully cradled the cat in my hands. I asked the jogger to open my car trunk and remove the things from a small box. Then I gently placed the cat in the box. He was in shock, so he probably could not feel the pain from his obvious injuries. "Kinda funny lookin', isn't he?" asked the jogger. I was annoyed by his question, but I had to admit that he was right. This cat looked peculiar. Not ugly, mind you. But he seemed to have a comical look on his face, even at such a dreadful time.

"What are you gonna do with him?" the jogger asked. I told him I would take the cat to the local vet and let him decide what to do.

The vet was only five minutes away. My wife and I had been bringing our animals to him for several years, and I knew I could rely on him to do what was best for the cat. I brought the cat into the reception room and placed it on the counter. As this was an emergency, the vet was summoned right away. He examined the cat thoroughly, listing the injuries for his assistant to write down. "Broken jaw, that'll have to be set. Two teeth broken. A couple more loose. Possible internal injuries, but they don't look too bad. Uh-oh. This doesn't look good. He doesn't appear to have any movement in his right front leg. Possible break, definite ligament and tendon damage."

The vet completed his examination, then looked at me and asked what I wanted to do. I knew what he meant. Did I want to have the cat "put to sleep"? I became uneasy. I clumsily explained that I was hoping to get advice from him on what to do. Fair enough. The jaw would have to be wired shut for six weeks, and the cat would have to wear a cast on its leg for three months. There was no way of knowing if the damage to the leg was permanent. He could have the cast removed and still not be able to use the leg. The cost of all the surgery would be high, but I would get a 50 percent "good Samaritan" discount if I went ahead with it.

Now I was really at a loss. If I went ahead with the surgery, I'd be paying for a cat which wasn't mine, whose owner I'd probably never find, and who might end up with the use of only three legs. And on top of it, this was one of the funniest-looking cats ever born. Black and white, spotted where it shouldn't be, twisted tail, and a silly half-smile on its face. I chuckled at that and the entire situation.

"What do you want to do, Bill?" asked the vet.

I shrugged my shoulders in resignation. "Dan, I'll choose life over death every time. Let's give it our best shot."

I called back later in the day and learned that the surgery had been successful. "You can pick up your cat tomorrow morning," I was told. My cat. I started to say that he was not my cat, but I knew otherwise.

The next morning, my wife and I drove to the vet and picked up the cat. He looked ghastly. His jaw was now bandaged, and a cast covered one leg entirely and wrapped around his midsection. We were dejected. But, as we drove him home, we began thinking that perhaps this cat was not as pathetic as he looked. As frightened as he must have been, as much pain as he must have felt, he sat calmly in my wife's lap. He purred and stared out the window with his curious half-smile.

When we got home, we introduced him to our two Siamese cats, who stared in disbelief at this strange creature. They sensed it might be a cat, but they had never seen one like this. It took him very little time to get used to his new surroundings. It took him longer to get used to the cast, which made even walking a chore. Surely he must have been embarrassed. After all, an animal normally able to glide around quietly should not make a resounding thump every time he moves.

In due time, the cast came off. To our relief, Pokey, as we now called him, had about 90 percent mobility in the leg. He got around okay, but he limped whenever he tried to move any faster than a slow walk.

All this occurred four years ago. Pokey is still with us today. In fact, he has become our most beloved cat. Because of his injury, he is strictly an indoor cat. This does not seem to bother him at all. It is hard to believe that any cat has ever enjoyed himself more. Maybe it's because he had been slowed after being hit by a car, or perhaps he just has a special individuality. He is never bored. At times he will race around the house like he is leading the Indy 500. Or he'll leap into the air at an imaginary foe. Or he'll purr loudly at the foot of our bed, staring into space with that silly grin on his face. And he couldn't care less that he still looks funny.

It would have been easy to let Pokey lie in the middle of the road. And it would have been just as simple to have the vet put him to sleep. But when I think of all the pleasure this cat has given us, and of how much fun he has living with us, I know the right decision was made. And I'd do it again in a second. I'll take life over death every time.

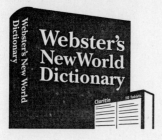

## PREVIEW

Here is a true story about a person with a learning disability—she was unable to read for almost twenty years. Being good at math, she was passed on from one grade to the next. Although she was able to get a good job after high school, her difficulties with reading made life difficult. Eventually, she decided it was better to face her problem and conquer it. This is Marvel Kretzmann's success story.

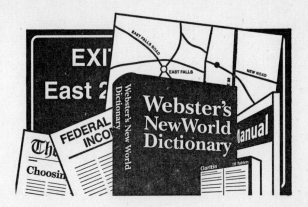

# BECOME A READER

*Mary Sherry*

Imagine a world where you can't read the street signs. You have to find your way by using only landmarks. When you see a sign or road map, you can't understand it, even though it is written in your own language. And when people give you oral directions, you cannot write quickly enough to take useful notes.

In this world, getting around isn't your only challenge. You must struggle to read directions on packages of cake mixes and cleaning products. Figuring out the doses of over-the-counter medicines actually gives you a headache. You keep faulty products rather than return them to the store because you cannot fill out a refund slip. The only jobs you dare apply for are those that do not require any reading or writing.

This was Marvel Kretzmann's world for almost twenty years. It was a very small world because she feared getting lost if she went beyond her place of work, familiar stores, and well-known routes to friends' and family's homes. She lived in daily fear that she would be asked to fill out a form or write something down for someone. Her world was a terrifying place.

Marvel's greatest fear of all was being found out. What if people knew that she could barely read and couldn't write at all?

Marvel was in the fifth grade when it became clear to her that she was far behind her classmates in reading and writing, and that she would never be able to catch up.

"I remember hearing giggles in the class-room as soon as I was called on to read out loud. The kids knew what was going to happen, and so did I. Any word with an "s" sound in it was sure to make me stumble. As I hesitated, my teacher would say the words for me, over and over, urging me to repeat after her. But all I could hear was the laughing in the background.

"Finally, the teacher would give up and say,

'We'll move on.' Even though I felt relief, I also felt embarrassed. I was pulled out of class for extra work, but by that time—as I realize now—it was too late. I was already labeled by classmates and teachers as 'slow.'

"But I was pretty good in math. This helped me get passed from grade to grade. It also helped me to hide how serious my problem was from my parents. I didn't want to bring the problem to their attention. As a ten-year-old, I was more interested in having fun than working hard on reading and writing."

Marvel had two close friends who accepted her for what she was, and is today: kind, generous, and a lot of fun. They would take notes for her and coach her through courses, and they helped cover her disability.

But those friends couldn't be with her all the time. Marvel recalls how in the large junior and senior high schools she attended, classmates soon caught on to her problem when the teacher asked students to take turns reading out loud. "Come on! Hurry up! She can't read!" she heard kids saying under their breath. Soon, rather than calling on students in order, up and down rows, teachers would skip around the class. That way, they wouldn't have to call on Marvel.

"In high school I learned to avoid classes

that had writing assignments and heavy reading. I took the easiest courses I could. I kept quiet and tried not to be noticed. I never volunteered in class. I earned the reputation of being a 'good' child. So many classes had multiple-choice tests that I usually could guess and get by. In fact, I remember one time when I was the only one in my class to get an A on an exam. I just did what I always did with those tests I couldn't understand. I went down the pages and marked this one or that one, guessing all the way!"

Marvel's ability to manage her life got better and better. She received her high-school diploma and enrolled in a technical school where she was trained as a dental assistant. A tutor helped her get through her classes. After finishing the program, she found a job. She liked being a dental assistant and discovered she was good at it. In this job she was safe! She didn't have to write or read instructions to do her work.

Life outside of the dental office was another matter. Things she bought, such as appliances and other household items, came with instruction manuals. Expert at sewing, Marvel bought a fairly complicated sewing machine. "I thought I was going to lose my mind threading it and adjusting the tension. There were instructions in the manual, but they might as well have been in a foreign language.

"When I bought a computer, I practically burned out the phone lines dialing everyone I thought might be able to help me. I called the computer salesperson, friends, my sister, and 1-800-SOS-APPL day and night. I simply couldn't read the manual well enough to understand the computer's most basic uses. I would call and nervously ask, 'Why is this thing beeping at me? What did I do?' I needed to be walked through each disaster so I could keep on going."

The opportunities—and pitfalls—of the adult world seemed endless, requiring new and more complicated adjustments. Marvel wanted a checking account. Getting one was easy, because the bank officer simply asked her questions and filled out the forms. Marvel discovered, though, that writing out checks was stressful, especially when she had to do it in public. She developed a system of filling in store names on the checks at home or in the car before shopping—just so she wouldn't have to struggle in front of a clerk. Since spelling out "eleven" and "twelve" was always troubling, Marvel simply avoided writing checks for those amounts. As she shopped, she ran totals of her purchases in her head. Then she bought additional items or put some back on the shelves, just so the bill would be at least thirteen dollars or less than eleven.

Marvel's husband knew she had difficulty reading and writing, but he had no idea just how much difficulty. He knew she had never been an "A" student, but he realized that she could manage things. For example, she addressed their wedding invitations from carefully printed lists. She wrote a form letter for her thank-you notes. Whenever a gift arrived, she copied that letter, simply filling in the blank for whatever the gift was. She had a "system," and it worked.

But sometimes she got caught. A few years ago Marvel won a radio contest sponsored by an insurance company. The prize was a free luncheon for all the people in her office at a restaurant of Marvel's choice. She stopped by a popular spot to check it out, thinking it would be a nice place to treat her fellow workers. A restaurant employee asked her to write down the name and address of the business so she could send a menu to Marvel's office. Marvel couldn't remember how to spell "Chicago"—the name of the street where her office is located. "I just blocked," she said. "I see 'Chicago' written out many times every day, but at that moment I froze. I turned and walked out—feeling defeated by such a simple thing as spelling 'Chicago.' I arranged to have the luncheon somewhere else."

Marvel Kretzmann tells about her struggle almost as though she were talking about someone else. She is upbeat, self-confident, poised, open, and very friendly. Now in her late thirties, she realizes that difficulty reading and writing is a fairly widespread problem. "There are a lot of us out there," she says. "There are people who are afraid to travel because they can't read signs. Some won't apply for work because they can't fill out a job application. Others pretend they have left their glasses at home so they can take a form to someone who will read it to them. What is sad, though, is that many people assume people like us are lazy because we won't write things down in front of them. Sometimes when they see us struggle, they think we simply don't concentrate, or worse, that we are worthless. Once when I applied for a job, the person who interviewed me corrected my job application in front of me! Imagine how I felt! I told myself I couldn't work for that man, even if he offered me a job."

This remarkable openness and confidence did not come about by accident, nor did they come easily. After all, Marvel had spent years and years ashamed of her difficulty. How did she build her self-esteem to such a high level? "I suddenly came face to face with the reality that life wasn't going to get any easier! In fact, it was getting harder." Marvel and her husband had bought a house, and she couldn't understand the legal papers involved. Furthermore, Marvel could see changes coming to the dental profession. One day her job would require taking notes and filling out forms. The thought also occurred to her that since she has no children, there might not be anyone around to take care of her when she was old or to cover for her when she needed help with reading or writing.

So Marvel decided to go back to school.

She found a community adult-education program that offered brush-up classes in academic subjects. There she found just what she needed and received small-group and individual instruction. The work was intense. Teachers trained to deal with special learning needs drilled Marvel in phonics, spelling, and reading. Marvel came to school right after work and usually got there before the teachers did. The staff members who arrived first always found Marvel deep in study in the hallway. Finally they gave her a key to the classroom!

According to her teacher, Marvel's difficulties are typical of learning-disabled students. Such a person has a normal or an above-normal IQ, but for some reason is unable to process math or reading and spelling. Unfortunately, the problem often isn't identified until the student is well beyond the grade levels where it could and should be more easily addressed. The problem is made worse by youthful reactions, such as bad behavior—or, in Marvel's case, extremely good behavior—and covering up.

Marvel is unhappy that she slipped through the system. "As an adult I can see there were great gaps in communications between my teachers and my parents—and between me and my teachers, and me and my parents on this issue! I fell through all the cracks. My teachers failed to impress on my parents very early on that I was having trouble. I didn't want my parents to think I wasn't doing well. And I didn't have the guts to approach the teachers and say, 'Hey!' There were times I felt no teacher cared, as long as I didn't disrupt the class."

Marvel doesn't think much about the past, though. She is mastering her computer—by reading the instructions. She plans to attend school for another year or so to keep working on spelling and writing, "to keep it fresh." Since she went back to school five years ago, her reading has risen from the fourth-grade level to a level beyond high school.

Writing is still a chore, and reading is work, too. "I'm never going to write a book," Marvel says. "I can't even read a three-hundred-page novel in a week—it might take me a month or two. But that doesn't bother me. I know I have made real progress when I can set small goals and achieve them. I was so proud one time when my husband asked me to read a manual to him while he worked on my car. He looked up from under the hood and told me I was doing a great job and that school was really helping me!

"Thankfully, I can write letters now and make lists for shopping and for packing for vacations. I can take notes and write memos to others and know they will be understood. I have learned to use a lot of tools, including a dictionary, a thesaurus (which I never knew existed), and a computer. I have also learned I need lots of quiet time to do these things well.

"I am able to read newspapers, magazine articles, and instruction manuals, even out loud if the situation calls for it. I feel more confident reading stories to my nieces and nephews and my friends' children. These are tremendous rewards—all the rewards I really need to make me feel good about going back to school.

"It hasn't been easy, despite all the wonderful help I've had. I will never forget my first night in a writing class after going to school for reading and phonics for a couple of years. The writing teacher gave the students fifteen minutes to write a short description about their favorite place. I could think of lots of places I would love to tell people about, but I couldn't write anything more than my name at the top of the paper! After the class my teacher and I agreed I wasn't ready for this yet. I didn't feel defeated, though. I returned to the phonics and reading group. A few months later I went back. By then I was able to handle the writing class. This class was another turning point for me. My teacher helped me break the silence. At last I was able to speak freely about the secret I had been hiding all these years. Now I feel good about writing something down and then reading it out loud."

Marvel believes it is important for her to encourage others who share her disability. "In the School for Adults, my teachers have asked me to reach out to people who they know have the same problem. I can spot them, too. They don't talk to anyone, they keep their heads buried in books they are struggling to read, and they never mix with the other students. Sometimes when I approach people who need a lot of help, they turn away because they don't want to admit how bad their problem is. I know how they feel. I also know that it is by taking many small steps that they will make progress. There are no miracles here, just a lot of hard work!

"Occasionally I am asked to speak to small groups about the School for Adults and how it helped me to meet this challenge. Sometimes I feel uncomfortable and feel I'm saying, in effect, 'Hi, I'm Marvel, and I am illiterate!' However, I believe it is important to do what I can to get the word out to others who may benefit from the program.

"When school was ending last spring, several people in our study work group asked me if I would organize a little class for them during the summer. I was floored! They were actually looking up to me! But I felt that if they thought I could help them, I knew they could push me, too, so why not? We met nearly every week and practiced reading out loud, and we worked on pronunciation and word definitions."

How far has Marvel come? Not long ago she was invited to serve on the Advisory Council for the School for Adults. She sits as an equal with the school's director, teacher representatives, business owners, and others from the community.

At one meeting, the secretary was absent, and the chairman asked if someone would take notes for her. Without a moment's thought, Marvel said, "I will."

And she did!

**COLLEGE SURVIVAL KIT**

## PREVIEW

Sometimes the best teacher is a student. That is certainly the case with Jean Coleman, whose experience as a community-college student has given her a wealth of experience to share with others. You won't find the kind of insight Coleman has in any school or college catalog. She has gained it the hard way—through experience—and offers it as a gift to you.

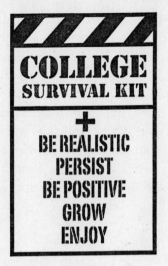

**COLLEGE
SURVIVAL KIT**

+

BE REALISTIC
PERSIST
BE POSITIVE
GROW
ENJOY

# LEARNING
# SURVIVAL SKILLS

*Jean Coleman*

For four years I was a student at a community college. I went to night school as a part-time student for three years, and I was able to be a full-time student for one year. My first course was a basic writing course because I needed a review of grammar and the basics of writing. I did well in that course, and that set the tone for everything that followed.

It is now eleven years since I started college, and I have a good job with a Philadelphia accounting firm. When I was invited to write this article, the questions put to me were, "What would you want to say to students who are just starting out in college? What advice would you give? What experiences would it help to share?" I thought a lot about what it took for me to be a successful student. Here, then, are my secrets for survival in college and, really, for survival in life as well.

## "Be Realistic."

The first advice that I'd give to beginning students is: "Be realistic about how college will help you get a job." Some students believe that once they have college degrees the world will be waiting on their doorsteps, ready to give them wonderful jobs. But the chances are that unless they've planned, there will be nobody on their doorsteps.

I remember the way my teacher in a study-skills course dramatized this point in class. He pretended to be a student who had just been handed a college degree. He opened up an imaginary door, stepped through, and peered around in both directions outside. There was nobody to be seen. I understood the point he was making immediately. A college degree in itself isn't enough. We've got to prepare while we're in college to make sure our degree is a marketable one.

At that time I began to think seriously about (1) what I wanted to do in life and (2) whether there were jobs out there for what I wanted to do. I went to the counseling center and said, "I want to learn where the best job opportunities will be in the next ten years." The counselor referred me to a copy of the Occupational Outlook Handbook published by the United States government. The Handbook has good information on what kinds of jobs are available now and which career fields will need workers in the future. In the front of the book is a helpful section on job hunting. The counselor also gave me a vocational interest test to see where my skills and interests lay.

The result of my personal career planning was that I eventually graduated from community college with a degree in accounting. I then got a job almost immediately, for I had chosen an excellent employment area. The firm that I work for paid my tuition as I went on to get my bachelor's degree. It is now paying for my work toward certification as a certified public accountant, and my salary increases regularly.

By way of contrast, I know a woman named Sheila who earned a bachelor's degree with honors in French. After graduation, she spent several unsuccessful months trying to find a job using her French degree. Sheila eventually wound up going to a specialized school where she trained for six months as a paralegal assistant. She then got a job on the strength of that training—but her years of studying French were of no practical value in her career at all.

I'm not saying that college should serve only as a training ground for a job. People should take some courses just for the sake of learning and for expanding their minds in different directions. At the same time, unless they have an unlimited amount of money (and few of us are so lucky), they must be ready at some point to take career-oriented courses so that they can survive in the harsh world outside.

In my own case, I started college at the age of twenty-seven. I was divorced, had a six-year-old son to care for, and was working full time as a hotel night clerk. If I had had my preference, I would have taken a straight liberal arts curriculum. As it was, I did take some general-interest courses—in art, for example. But mainly I was getting ready for the solid job I desperately needed. I am saying, then, that students must be realistic. If they will need a job soon after graduation, they should be sure to study in an area where jobs are available.

## "Persist."

The older I get, the more I see that life lays on us some hard experiences. There are times for each of us when simple survival becomes a deadly serious matter. We must then learn to persist—to struggle through each day and wait for better times to come—as they always do.

I think of one of my closest friends, Neil. After graduating from high school with me, Neil spent two years working as a stock boy at a local department store in order to save money for college tuition. He then went to the guidance office at the small college in our town. Incredibly, the counselor there told him, "Your IQ is not high enough to do college work." Thankfully, Neil decided to go anyway and earned his degree in five years—with a year out to care for his father, who had had a stroke one day at work.

Neil then got a job as a manager of a regional beauty-supply firm. He met a woman who owned a salon, got married, and soon had two children. Three years later he found out that his wife was having an affair. I'll never forget the day Neil came over and sat at my kitchen table and told me what he had learned. He always seemed so much in control, but that morning he lowered his head into his hands and cried.

"What's the point?" he kept saying in a low voice over and over to himself.

But Neil has endured. He divorced his wife, won custody of his children, and learned how to be a single parent. Recently, Neil and I got letters informing us of the twentieth reunion of our high-school graduating class. Included was a short questionnaire for us to fill out that ended with this item: "What has been your outstanding accomplishment since graduation?" Neil wrote, "My outstanding accomplishment is that I have survived." I have a feeling that many of our high-school classmates, twenty years out in the world, would have no trouble understanding the truth of his statement.

I can think of people who started college with me who had not yet learned, like Neil, the basic skill of endurance. Life hit some of them with unexpected low punches and knocked them to the floor. Stunned and dismayed, they didn't fight back and eventually dropped out of school. I remember Yvonne, still a teenager, whose parents involved her in their ugly divorce battle. Yvonne started missing classes and gave up at midsemester. There was Alan, whose girlfriend broke off their relationship. Alan stopped coming to class, and by the end of the semester he was failing most of his courses. I also recall

Nelson, whose old car kept breaking down. After Nelson put his last two hundred dollars into it, the brakes failed and needed to be replaced. Overwhelmed by his continuing car troubles, Nelson dropped out of school. And there was Rita, discouraged by her luck of the draw with teachers and courses. In sociology, she had a teacher who wasn't able to express ideas clearly. She also had a mathematics teacher who talked too fast and seemed not to care at all about whether his students learned. To top it off, Rita's adviser had enrolled her in an economics course that put her to sleep. Rita told me she had expected college to be an exciting place, but instead she was getting busywork assignments and trying to cope with hostile or boring teachers. Rita decided to drop her mathematics course, and that must have set something in motion in her head, for she soon dropped her other courses as well.

In my experience, younger students seem more likely to drop out than do older students. I think some younger students are still in the process of learning that life slams people around without warning. I'm sure they feel that being knocked about is especially unfair because the work of college is hard enough without having to cope with other hardships.

In some situations, withdrawing from college may be the best response. But there are going to be times in college when students—young or old—must simply determine, "I am going to persist." They should remember that no matter how hard their lives may be, there are many other people out there who are quietly having great difficulties also. I think of Dennis, a boy in my introductory psychology class who lived mostly on peanut butter and discount-store white bread for almost a semester in his freshman year. And I remember Estelle, who came to school because she needed a job to support her sons when her husband, who was dying of leukemia, would no longer be present. These are especially dramatic examples of the faith and hope that are sometimes necessary for us to persist.

### "Be Positive."

A lot of people are their own worst enemies. They regard themselves as unlikely to succeed in college and often feel that there have been no accomplishments in their lives. In my first year of college especially, I saw people get down on themselves all too quickly. There were two students in my developmental mathematics class who failed the first quiz and seemed to give up immediately. From that day on, they walked into the classroom carrying defeat on their shoulders the way other students carried textbooks under their arms. I'd look at them slouching in their seats, not even taking notes, and think, "What terrible things have gone on in their lives that they have quit already? They have so little faith in their ability to learn that they're not even trying." Both students hung on until about midsemester. When they disappeared for good, no one took much notice, for they had already disappeared in spirit after that first test.

They are not the only people in whom I have seen the poison of self-doubt do its ugly work. I have seen others with surrender in their eyes and have wanted to shake them by the shoulders and say, "You are not dead. Be proud and pleased that you have brought yourself here to college. Many people would not have gotten so far. Be someone. Breathe. Hope. Act." Such people should refuse to use self-doubts as an excuse for not trying. They should roll up their sleeves and get to work. They should start taking notes in class and trying to learn. They should get a tutor, go to the learning center, see a counselor. If they honestly and fully try and still can't handle a course, only then should they drop it. Above all, they should not lapse into being "zombie students"—ones who have given up in their heads but persist in hanging on for months, going through hollow motions of trying.

Nothing but a little time is lost through being positive and giving school your best shot. On the other hand, people who let self-doubts limit their efforts may lose the opportunity to test their abilities to the fullest.

## "Grow."

I don't think that people really have much choice about whether to grow in their lives. To not be open to growth is to die a little each day. Grow or die—it's as simple as that.

I have a friend, Jackie, who, when she's not working, can almost always be found at home or at her mother's house. Jackie eats too much and watches TV too much. I sometimes think that when she swings open her apartment door in response to my knock, I'll be greeted by her familiar chubby body with an eight-inch-screen television set occupying the place where her head used to be.

Jackie seems quietly desperate. There is no growth or plan for growth in her life. I've said to her, "Go to school and study for a job you'll be excited about." She says, "It'll take me forever." Once Jackie said to me, "The favorite time of my life was when I was a teenager. I would lie on my bed listening to music and I would dream. I felt I had enormous power, and there seemed no way that life would stop me from realizing my biggest dreams. Now that power doesn't seem possible to me anymore."

I feel that Jackie must open some new windows in her life. If she does not, her spirit is going to die. There are many ways to open new windows, and college is one of them. For this reason, I think people who are already in school should stay long enough to give it a chance. No one should turn down lightly such an opportunity for growth.

### "Enjoy."

I hope I'm not making the college experience sound too grim. It's true that there are some hard, cold realities in life, and I think people need to plan for those realities. But I want to describe also a very important fact—that college is often a wonderful experience. There were some tough times when it would have been easy to just give up and quit, like the week when my son's babysitter broke her arm and my car's radiator blew up. If school had not been something I really enjoyed, I would not have made it.

To begin with, I realized soon after starting

college that almost no one there knew me. That might seem like a depressing thought, but that's not how it felt. I knew that people at college had not made up their minds about what kind of person Jean Coleman was. I imagined myself as shy, clumsy, and average. But in this new environment, I was free to present myself in any way I chose. I decided from my first week in school that my college classmates and instructors were going to see the new, improved Jean. I projected a confidence I didn't always feel. I sat near the front in every class. I participated, even took the lead, in discussions. Instead of slipping away after class, I made a point to chat with my teachers and invite other students to have coffee with me. Soon I realized that my "act" had worked. People regarded me as a confident, outgoing woman. I really liked this new image of myself as a successful college student.

Another of the pleasures of college was the excitement of walking into a class for the first time. At that point, the course was still just a name in a catalog. The possibilities for it seemed endless. Maybe the course would be a magic one sweeping me off my feet. Maybe the instructor would be really gifted in opening students' minds to new thoughts. Maybe through this course I would discover potential in myself

I never knew existed. I went into a new class ready to do everything I could—through my listening, participation, and preparation—to make it a success. And while some courses were more memorable than others, I rarely found one that didn't have some real rewards to offer me.

I even enjoyed the physical preparation for a new class. I loved going to the bookstore and finding the textbooks I'd need. I liked to sit down with them, crack open their binding and smell their new-book scent. It was fun to leaf through a textbook and see what seemed like difficult, unfamiliar material, realizing that in a few weeks I'd have a better grasp of what I was seeing there. I made a habit of buying a new spiral-bound notebook for each of my classes, even if I had others that were only partially used. Writing the new course's name on the notebook cover and seeing those fresh, blank sheets waiting inside helped me feel organized and ready to tackle a new challenge. I was surprised how many other students I saw scribbling their class notes on anything handy. I always wondered how they organized them to review later.

Surely one of the best parts of returning to school was the people I've met. Some of them became friends I hope I'll keep forever; others were passing acquaintances, but all of them have made my life richer. One of the best friends I made is a woman named Charlotte. She was my age, and she, like me, came back to school after her marriage broke up. I first met Charlotte in a basic accounting class, and she was scared to death. She was convinced that she could never keep up with the younger students and was sure she had made a big mistake returning to college. Since I often felt that way myself, Charlotte and I decided to become study partners. I'll never forget one day about three weeks into the term when I found her standing in the hallway after class, staring as if into space. "Charlotte?" I said, and she turned to me and broke into a silly grin. "Jean, I get it!" she exclaimed, giving me a quick hug. "I just realized I was sitting there in class keeping up as well as anyone else. I can do this!" Seeing Charlotte's growing confidence helped me believe in my own ability to succeed.

I found that I was looked to as an "older, wiser woman" by many of my classmates. And while I didn't pretend to have all of the answers, I enjoyed listening to their concerns and helping them think about solutions. My advice to them probably wasn't much different from what other adults might have said—take college seriously, don't throw away the opportunities you have, don't assume finding "the right person" is going to solve all the problems of life, and start planning for a career now. But somehow they seemed to find listening to such advice easier when it came from me, a fellow student.

Getting to know my instructors was a pleasure, as well. I remember how I used to think about my high-school teachers—that they existed only between nine and three o'clock and that their lives involved nothing but teaching us chemistry or social studies. But I got to know many of my college instructors as real people and even as friends. I came to think of my instructors as my partners, working together with me to achieve my goals. They weren't perfect or all-knowing—they were just people, with their own sets of problems and shortcomings. But almost all were people who really cared about helping me get where I wanted to go.

## In Conclusion

Maybe I can put all I've said into a larger picture by describing briefly what my life is like now. I have many inner resources that I did not have when I was just divorced. I have a secure future with the accounting firm where I work. My son is doing OK in school. I have friends. I am successful and proud and happy. I have my fears and my loneliness and my problems and my pains, but essentially I know that I have made it. I have survived and done more than survive. I am tough, not fragile, and I can rebound if hard blows land. I feel passionately that all of us can control our own destinies. I urge every beginning student to use well the chances that college provides. Students should plan for a realistic career, get themselves organized, learn to persist, be positive, and open themselves to growth. In such ways, they can help themselves find happiness and success in this dangerous but wonderful world of ours.

# AFTERWORD

Have you ever noticed the caption that sometimes flashes on at the beginning of a TV show or movie: "BASED ON A TRUE STORY"?

Have you heard about people who've been through an unusual experience—maybe they've done something heroic, or survived a disaster—who have then "sold their story to Hollywood" or written a book?

When you were younger, did you ever ask an adult, "Tell me about when you were little"?

If you answer "yes" to any of these questions, you already know something about the appeal of the real-life story.

Sure, everyone enjoys a fictional (made-up) story once in a while. Fiction is fun because it's limited only by the author's imagination. In fiction, pigs can fly, aliens can descend to Earth, and people can travel back into time in order to change history.

But real-life stories—*non*-fiction—are at least as enjoyable in a different way. They can challenge us, or amuse us, or interest us, or anger us, or inspire us in a very personal way, *because they really happened to real people, like us.* We can identify with them in a way that isn't always possible with made-up stories. While fictional stories may deal with very unusual events, exotic locations, and unlikely circumstances, real-life stories are more likely to make us think, "I can relate to that. The person in this story could have been me."

The book you are holding, *Ten Real-Life Stories,* contains ten stories of that sort—real, non-fiction stories about real things that happened to real people. Two of those people are now famous: Dick Gregory is a well-known comedian and author, and Benjamin Carson is a world-renowned surgeon. The other eight are not. And in their stories, even Gregory and Carson are writing about things that happened in their childhoods, long before they were famous. In other words, these stories are not about celebrities or sports stars or the very rich. They are about people who might remind you of your friends, your neighbors, your relatives, or even your self.

The main characters in "The Yellow

Ribbon," for instance, are Vingo, an ex-convict on his way home to see his wife, and a young girl, a fellow passenger on the bus. As the two talk, the girl gets a very surprising glimpse into Vingo's life. The story may remind you of a conversation you've had with a stranger. Oddly enough, people are sometimes inspired to tell intimate details of their lives to strangers they never expect to see again. "The Yellow Ribbon" provides a real-life example of such a thing happening.

"Shame," "Rowing the Bus," and "The Scholarship Jacket," are three very different stories about three different people. And yet those people share some common characteristics. "Shame" is about Dick Gregory, a poor, fatherless black boy in elementary school. "Rowing the Bus" is about something that happened to Paul Logan when he was a poor, fatherless white boy, also in elementary school. And "The Scholarship Jacket" is about an event in the life of Marta Salinas, a poor Mexican-American girl, when she was in eighth grade. In each of their stories, Dick, Paul, and Marta face humiliation and discrimination. How they each deal with their experience, and what lessons they carry away, make their stories memorable.

"A Drunken Ride" is actually a news story

that originally appeared in the *Philadelphia Inquirer*. It tells the tragic true story of a group of high-school friends and their fatal decision to mix alcohol and driving. Reading it, almost any teenager can imagine it involving himself or herself, or his or her friends. The families of the boys involved allowed this story to be written, hoping it will convince other teens not to drink and drive.

The next two stories, "The Professor is a Dropout" and "Do It Better!" are similar in their messages. Each is about someone who had been labeled—one as "retarded," and the other as "the dumbest kid in the class"—who took matters into his or her own hands. The stories of Guadalupe Quintanilla and Ben Carson may inspire you to reject a label society might want to pin on you.

"Life Over Death" begins with the writer encountering a situation we've surely all been in. He sees a cat lying in the road, apparently dead. He makes a split-second decision that will affect his life—as well as the cat's!—for years to come.

Finally, "Becoming a Reader" and "Learning Survival Skills" tell real-life stories of students who encounter obstacles to their success, and how they deal with those obstacles. As these students' stories make clear, barriers to success come in all shapes and sizes. And yet, ultimately, the nature of the barrier is less important than the attitude of the student.

In *Ten Real-Life Stories,* you will read about events that may amuse you, sadden you, interest you, and even inspire you. As you enjoy these stories, keep in mind that every word in them is true. Maybe someday someone will be reading the story of *your* life. What would you like it to say?

## Acknowledgments

If you liked
*Ten Real-Life Stories*
you may be interested in
other true stories in the
Townsend Library.

*continued on the following pages*

# Everyday
# Heroes

Beth Johnson

*Narrative of the Life of*

# FREDERICK DOUGLASS

## An American Slave

Written by Himself

TP THE TOWNSEND LIBRARY

Booker T. Washington

# UP FROM SLAVERY:

*An Autobiography*

THE TOWNSEND LIBRARY

SHIRLEY RUSSAK WACHTEL

# THE STORY OF
# BLIMA

*A Holocaust Survivor*

**TP** THE TOWNSEND LIBRARY

It Couldn't Happen to Me:

Three
True
Stories
of
Teenage
Moms

Beth Johnson

TP THE TOWNSEND LIBRARY

# Surviving Abuse
## Four True Stories

Beth Johnson

TP THE TOWNSEND LIBRARY